THE NEW ELECTRONIC TRADERS

UNDERSTANDING WHAT IT TAKES TO MAKE THE JUMP TO ELECTRONIC TRADING

JONATHAN R. ASPATORE

Special Section on the Future of Electronic Trading
by Omar Amanat, CEO of TRADESCAPE.*com*

MCGRAW-HILL

NEW YORK • SAN FRANCISCO • WASHINGTON, D.C. • AUCKLAND • BOGOTÁ
CARACAS • LISBON • LONDON • MADRID • MEXICO CITY • MILAN
MONTREAL • NEW DELHI • SAN JUAN • SINGAPORE
SYDNEY • TOKYO • TORONTO

McGraw-Hill

A Division of The **McGraw·Hill** Companies

1 2 3 4 5 6 7 8 9 0 FBG/FBG 9 0 9 8 7 6 5 4 3 2 1 0 9

ISBN 0-07-135772-6

This book was designed, edited, and set in New Century Schoolbook and Copperplate by TopDesk Publishers' Group. *Printed and bound by* Quebecor Printing.

McGraw-Hill books are available at special quantity discounts to use as premiums and sales promotions, or for use in corporate training programs. For more information, please write to the Director of Special Sales, McGraw-Hill, 11 West 19th Street, New York, NY 10011. Or contact your local bookstore.

This publication is designed to provide accurate and authoritative information in regard to the subject matter covered. It is sold with the understanding that neither the author nor the publisher is engaged in rendering legal, accounting, or other professional service. If legal advice or other expert assistance is required, the services of a competent professional person should be sought.
—*From a Declaration of Principles jointly adopted by a Committee of the American Bar Association and a Committee of Publishers.*

 This book is printed on recycled, acid-free paper containing a minimum of 50% recycled, de-inked fiber.

For Rachel...You are my center...I adore you.

Contents

Disclaimer

The views expressed by the author are his own and do not reflect the views of TRADESCAPE.*com*, Inc. The information contained is not to be construed as investment advice, and any reliance thereupon is at the reader's own risk.

This book is intended to educate and entertain those who have an interest in trading, either personally or professionally. The life of a trader is unlike any other job in the world. The unbelievable speed at which money is made and lost produces instant millionaires and bankrupts others. As you read, you will see how easy it is to make and lose fortunes in the world of electronic trading. Those who have the skills and discipline to excel stand to capitalize in ways that have never before been possible for the individual trader.

The mental capacity and discipline of electronic traders are the main determinants of their success. While there are numerous books about how to play the electronic trading game, it is just as important to understand the psyche of top traders. Each trader has a different story about how they have succeeded. By learning from their mistakes and taking advantage of their secrets, you can implement your own winning strategy.

This book is not a substitute for learning the fundamentals of how to trade. There are many books that deal with the specific techniques used by successful traders. However, this book will actually take you inside the minds of the masters of the game. This special insight will be invaluable if and when you take the leap to becoming an electronic trader. Good luck!

ACKNOWLEDGMENT

Thank you to Alison Friedman, Sohail Khalid, Stephen Isaacs, and Jeffrey Cranes for all of your help and guidance that made this book possible. Special thanks also to River Communications and Spire Integrated Design.

1

ELECTRONIC TRADING OVERVIEW

THE EVOLUTION OF TRADING

Trading and investing have always existed in our society in some form or another. But interest in the stock market has boomed in recent years due to easier access to market information, lower trade commissions, and fast-growth stocks in the technology sector. The Internet in particular has brought a wealth of information to the fingertips of each individual, allowing investors to make better-educated decisions about buying stocks. By providing access to market news and charging very low commissions, first generation online brokerage firms have enabled thousands of Americans to take charge of their own accounts instead of using a brokerage.

Until recently, it was impractical, if not impossible, for an individual not employed by a Wall Street firm to gain access to the instruments needed to become a successful trader. For many years professional traders at the large and elite firms were the only ones to have access to most of the information and to the expensive technology needed to access the markets directly.

But technology has advanced at a staggering rate over the last few years and has helped bridge the gap between institutions and individual investors. The de-institutionalization of Wall Street provided individuals with more affordable equipment and easier access to the markets. The Internet has enabled Information to be easily accessible from almost anywhere, by anyone. People can gain access to and make use of the same data that Wall Street traders rely upon, all in the comfort of their own homes. This access to information, coupled with the burgeoning of online trading, has created a new category of investor that has never previously existed. The advent of ECNs now allows these individuals to buy or sell stocks without the cost or interference of a middleman". Unlike traditional brokering methods, ECNs enable traders to capitalize on the quick movements of a stock by getting the best possible price.

The less-than-helpful attitude of the brokerage community, slow to relinquish its control on the market, also forced the Securities and Exchange Commission (SEC) to make changes that would foster a more level playing field. The first change, in 1987, was the mandatory participation of market makers in the ECNs. This groundbreaking rule finally allowed customers to send their orders directly to the market and was the first major step in the advent of electronic trading. Although it took years to pass the rule, and even longer for technology to advance to where it was feasible for the individual investor to participate, investors and traders now have access to the same information that was once available to only a select few.

But perhaps the biggest driver of the electronic trading industry is the amazing rise of the Internet industry. Billions of dollars have been made from the creation of this new industry and electronic traders have reaped the benefits of increased information flow facilitated by the Internet.

Interest in the Internet has been a major factor in the increased volume of total shares being traded and in fueling the U.S. equity markets. It stands to reason that as interest in online trading continues to rise, the popularity of the electronic trading field will also increase.

THE REVOLUTION

Electronic trading is quickly becoming Wall Street's hottest new revolution. Technology is driving this opportunity by connecting individual buyers and sellers for the first time. The most intriguing part of electronic trading is that anyone can try and be successful. Every electronic trader has a unique history and career path: some went to Ivy League schools, others never made it to college; some trade full-time, others on the side. Yet all share the same passion: to trade and make a fortune!

It has usually been assumed that the easiest way to make millions on Wall Street has been to work for a blue-chip firm like Goldman Sachs, Morgan Stanley, or Merrill Lynch. These firms were thought to provide the necessary tools, connections, and capital base to give you an advantage over others. Recent regulatory changes and advancements in technology have leveled the playing field and extended the opportunity to make it big on Wall Street to the individual investor. Electronic trading has emerged as a plausible way for anyone to take a shot at making a successful career.

It is also becoming a full-time profession for more and more individuals. Those who have an appetite for the fast-paced trading culture and who enjoy market activity are the ones who stand to be rewarded most handsomely. The biggest difference between electronic traders and Wall Street traders working for institutions is that the former get to take home all of their earnings. This minor difference has been enough to convince many individuals to leave their jobs at big-name Wall Street firms and take their chance at trading for themselves. Those who are successful are truly masters of their own destiny.

THE STAKES

The value of stocks on the New York Stock Exchange and NASDAQ have grown exponentially over the last decade, insiders have been slow to relinquish power and profits to the general public. They have controlled billions of dollars worth of securities for many years, and have had the inside track on making millions for themselves, while limiting access to external sources. The SEC has fought long and hard to open the markets, and only recently has succeeded in forcing deregulation. Electronic traders and online investors have gradually carved away at the enormous fees and profits that these groups once made. For the first time, individual investors can trade off of the same information as professional traders on Wall Street. Electronic traders use this information to capitalize on split-second movements within volatile markets, like many of the Internet stocks, and profit from a trade. For the first time, the general public is trading with Wall Street and sharing in their wealth.

The possibilities have never been greater. With record levels of funds pouring into the markets, there is an unprecedented amount of volatility, especially in the technology sector, where stocks such as Amazon.com, Yahoo, and eBay have soared over the last year. Whereas normal investors are usually in stocks for months, even years, expecting the price of the stock to rise gradually over time, electronic traders can be in a stock for a matter of seconds, making money on the stock as it goes up and down throughout the day. The volatility in technology stocks has allowed electronic traders to capitalize on the incredible daily swings.

The wealth being generated by electronic traders has left many on Wall Street a bit put off. They do not believe that electronic trading is "for real," or even legal. However, the fact remains that electronic trading is a legitimate and potentially lucrative profession. By using systems that allow direct access to the markets, electronic traders are able to enter and exit the market quickly, creating their own profitable spreads. Many Wall Street traders have less than complimentary remarks for electronic traders, believing they decrease the potential profit of traditional traders.

It is impossible to ignore the swelling number of online investors who will soon have access to all the tools needed to become successful electronic traders. They will be able to trade much the same way as they currently invest online. The major difference is that they will have the opportunity not only to trade for long-term gains, but also to trade for intra-day gains. This will continue to level the playing field for all investors.

What we are seeing is the gradual erosion of the "elite few" on Wall Street; those who previously controlled the trading of most stocks. As government regulation and technological advancement have gradually chipped away at insider control, the opportunity now exists for others to capitalize on what had been hoarded for the last 30 plus years. Electronic traders have been quick to realize the opportunities presented and have been rewarded many times over for being the first ones to do so. These opportunities continue to exist and it's not too late to join them.

THE TRADERS

Electronic traders, like so many others, are hungry to make it big on Wall Street. They are also the new "hot shots" on the street, working as they please, and taking home all of their trading profits.

Suffice it to say, electronic traders have not gone unnoticed in the financial world. Some big-name, traditional firms look upon them with disdain, deriding the way they trade as careless and uninformed. Direct connectivity to the markets enables electronic traders to place trades that can take advantage of even 1/8 point movements, making electronic investors very different from normal online investors. They invest small trades, in 100-share increments, and anticipate very small stock movements where they can make quick profits or cut their losses. Through direct access to market information, they can see the relative strength of specific stocks and predict their movements with reasonable accuracy. While some electronic traders make up to 1000 trades a day, others wait patiently until they feel the tide has turned for a particular stock. Regardless, technology has enabled them to take advantage of even the smallest movements in a stock. Because the field has grown so much in the last couple of years, electronic traders can have a substantial impact on the price movement within a stock.

Many traditional traders feel that this influence plays a large part in artificially escalating the prices of stocks, and could eventually cause a crash. Others argue that electronic traders are responsible for increasing the general liquidity of the markets and serve as the engine that has driven the overall market higher. Still others take umbrage at the success of electronic traders, feeling that they take away the money that should be earned by the "professionals." In truth, electronic trading firms provide unprecedented opportunities to make it big on Wall Street while playing by your own rules.

Survival of the fittest is the name of the game on Wall Street, where each investor must seek out his own personal advantage over other traders and investors. Traders are always in search of arbitrage opportunities, situations where an imbalance in the market appears for a short period of time until it is naturally corrected and represents a chance to quickly make a lot of money. These are short-lived, rare situations which present the opportunity to make a profit. Electronic trading, however, is no longer just an arbitrage situation. Traditional traders, however, are slow to recognize this fact. It threatens their livelihood. The people that stand to benefit most from electronic trading are those who have previously not had access to market information or market professionals. As interest in electronic trading builds within Wall Street, many traditional traders will jump ship in order to take a shot at making it on their own.

Electronic trading requires incredible discipline and a keen interest in the markets. On the other end of every trade is an individual or institution willing to take the flip side of your bet. There is no love lost on Wall Street where fortunes are made and lost at the push of a button. The excitement this creates, however, cannot be replicated anywhere else. Those who remain patient and adhere to their strategy of being disciplined will have a shot at making it big.

THE MARKETS

Most electronic traders choose to trade stocks on the Nasdaq because they are heavily traded and tend to be extremely volatile. The more a stock moves, the more opportunity there is to make money. The markets move so quickly that an opportunity that exists one second can vanish a few seconds later. The hands of an experienced electronic trader glide easily across the keyboard, absorbing information from all directions, quickly entering and exiting trades, taking a quick spread wherever they can. Every keystroke is critical, both in terms of accuracy and speed. The rise in volume of total shares traded over the last year has greatly increased the volatility of the market as a whole. This is especially true in the technology sector where stocks can move in a range of 10 to 40 points over a single day. For example, a stock such as Yahoo! may be up five points for the day, but it may have started down ten, risen 25 points, and then dropped ten to finish at 5 points above. These daily jumps represent chances to make profits much greater than just a five-point gain at the end of the day. The market is always changing, and those who have the speed, intuition, and nerve to play can learn how to make those changes work for them.

THE ELECTRONIC TRADING CULTURE

The dynamic atmosphere that exists on a trading floor creates an unmistakable edge in each individual who participates. Traders glue themselves to their screens, searching for any news that could impact the momentum of their stocks. Most electronic traders enjoy working in the company of their fellow traders, sharing information and basking in their freshly-earned wealth or woes. As a result, the trading floor of any firm tends to take on a personality of its own.

Electronic traders can now access the markets from almost anywhere via a laptop and an Internet connection. Some prefer to work out of their homes or on the road. In any trading environment, however, the rush of adrenaline is almost palpable. Each trader is focused on his own world, looking for the right pieces of news to consider and act upon accordingly in his trades. This is especially true for electronic traders, most of whom are trading with their own money.

SPLIT-SECOND FRENZY

The split-second frenzy of electronic trading is not unlike that of a video game. As an electronic trader quickly enters and exits a stock, absorbing massive amounts of information and calculating its momentum, his "score" fluctuates in the upper right hand corner of the screen, indicating how much money he has made or lost. Nonetheless, many electronic traders love what they do because of the fast-paced rush it provides.

Electronic traders need heavy volume to make money. The opportunity to make money is present only when a stock moves; the difficult part is timing a trade accurately so that you can capitalize on the 1/8 spread that may only exist for 10 to 20 seconds. Seasoned traders can seize this opportunity and then short the stock as it begins to decline. The sheer volume being traded in the U.S. equity markets over the past few years has made things especially interesting. It has created unprecedented volatility in stock prices. Internet stocks and IPOshave been known to rise over 50 percent of their market capitalization during the course of a day, creating previously unheard of opportunities for electronic traders to capitalize on the wild swings in these highly liquid stocks

TOOLS TO SUCCEED

The mental capacity and composure of the electronic trader are his most critical tools. Those traders who develop a trading strategy and have the discipline to stick to it stand a much greater chance of keeping their focus and making profitable trades. Taking the emotion out of the decision-making process enables them to make steady profits on a daily basis. Although intuition is a major part of trading stocks, traders who are tempted to deviate from their prescribed strategy run the risk of losing perspective and, as a result, their money. Any good electronic trader will advise remaining completely devoted to a predetermined strategy, especially in the heat of battle. In the end, this will pay off.

It can be painful for a trader to watch a stock rise another whole point right after he has sold it. But a savvy trader might recognize this as another smart time to buy. When caught waiting for a loser to rebound, it is easy to get deeper and deeper into a hole. This is one of the most costly mistakes a beginning electronic trader can make. Not only can it be financially devastating, but it serves to dampen morale as well. Most veteran electronic traders have very cut-and-dry enter- and-exit strategies to which they adhere strictly over the course of each trading day, updating their strategies as the markets change over time.

Two tangible resources that any successful electronic trader must have at his command are direct access to breaking market news and direct access to trading stocks. Tools such as real-time quotes and Nasdaq level-II screens, which display the groups actively trading the stock, allow electronic traders to gauge the momentum of individual stocks and capitalize on quick movements.

Having the proper tools greatly increases an electronic trader's chance for success. So much of becoming a successful electronic trader is dependent on mental capacity and discipline. Being able to comprehend volumes of information at the blink of an eye in order to determine the next movement of a stock takes concentration, intuition, and hard work. Successful electronic traders make full use of all of the resources at their disposal, which gives them an edge in the markets.

HOW TO SUCCEED

In order to become an electronic trader, you must have direct access to the markets. The implementation of Electronic Communication Networks (ECNs) has narrowed the spread for stocks considerably. Traders can now quickly enter and exit markets to act immediately on a quoted price for a stock, at only a fraction of the price that it would have cost them just a few years ago.

Each electronic trader trades a little differently from his fellow traders. Some set limits on their losses and let their winners run; others follow a very regimented strategy of getting in and out of positions within seconds, hoping for a two point gain and no more than a 1/2 point loss. Some electronic traders invest for a slightly longer time period: a couple of hours or even a day. Most electronic traders trade in highly liquid stocks, usually those that are traded on the Nasdaq, and in increments of anywhere from 100 to 1,000 shares a trade.

Good traders find it easy to predict the movements of stocks. It may not be any one particular sign, but a combination of intangibles that leads to an understanding of which direction the stock will move in next. The U.S. equity markets are in a constant state of change; therefore, it is important for every investor to be consistently updating his trading style. These changes may occur once a year, or once every ten years, but the key is to be able to recognize when the market is in the midst of a revision, and to update your strategy accordingly.

It can take months before an electronic trader understands the momentum of the market and is able to gauge the movement of individual stocks. Like trying to drive a manual car for the first time, once you have practiced for a while it becomes a lot easier. In order to get beginners started off on the right foot, several electronic trading firms supply their new hires with the capital to start their careers. But becoming a successful electronic trader does not happen overnight and most start with their own money. Understanding the fundamentals of what moves individual stocks involves a significant learning period. Even the most successful electronic traders are only right 50 to 60 percent of the time. However, this is enough to earn a handsome profit on a daily basis.

CONCLUSIONS

There has never before been a profession like electronic trading on Wall Street. In the past, opportunities such as these on Wall Street evaporated before they could be fully realized by the general public. Although there is no telling when the window of opportunity for electronic trading might close, it does not appear to be anywhere in the near future. The government regulations that have finally been forced upon the markets have made it possible for everyone to have a hand in the game and cash in on the billions of dollars of trading profits earned annually. Although many feel that electronic trading must be gambling, the fact is there could be nothing further from the truth. Outsiders are afraid of what they don't understand. The American public has been kept in the dark about access to the financial markets for so long, it is slow to comprehend the opportunities that have emerged, now that the playing field has leveled.

For those who choose to capitalize on this opportunity, there is nothing like the excitement of fitting together the puzzle of how world news, market information, and general consumer sentiment will determine the movement of a stock. It is the ultimate way to test one's skills against the rest of the investment world. By trading purposefully and taking the time to learn about what drives individual stocks, you can create opportunities for success on Wall Street. Best of all, your wealth can be accrued on your own terms and in your own time. Forget about the naysayers who say you can't make money until you've retired at age 60. The following interviews and stories will give you first-hand insight into the minds of some of the most successful electronic traders and their winning ways.

2

THE INTERNET REVOLUTION

—*John Cassimatis*

U NLIKE SOME TRADERS, JOHN CASSIMATIS WILL HOLD A STOCK FOR DAYS,
WEEKS, OR EVEN MONTHS, AS LONG AS IT HAS SOMETHING TO DO WITH
THE INTERNET, WHICH HE BELIEVES WILL BE THE FOUNDATION OF OUR ECONO-
MY IN THE CENTURY TO COME. HE NEVER BUYS STOCKS IN OTHER INDUSTRIES.
INSTEAD, HE CONCENTRATES ON UNDERSTANDING THE PERSONALITY, HISTORY,
AND MOVEMENT OF A FEW INTERNET STOCKS, A STRATEGY THAT HAS WORKED
FOR HIM SINCE HE STARTED TRADING IN MAY 1996.

What is the best way to get into electronic trading?

If you want to become an electronic trader, you have to make
a full-time commitment to learning about a particular industry or group of stocks. At the minimum, you must commit to
trading on a regular basis during a certain time of the day.
Stocks tend to move the most during the first and last two

hours of the trading day. The key is to try and piece together market news and information to understand the movement of particular stocks. Every tick of a stock is part of the story and part of its personality. By carefully watching a stock over time, you begin to see patterns and understand its movements. Just as important is understanding how other investors and traders react to specific market news.

What is a good way for a new electronic trader to begin making trades?

Over time you will learn the best and quickest way to buy a stock. Electronic traders have four major ways to buy a stock: Island, InstaNet, SelectNet, and SOES. These different systems are all ways to make a trade directly with another party. There is no middleman, so when you press enter, your trade is executed almost instantaneously. Each ECN system has a different level of volume and different types of traders trading on it, so you need to be looking at all of the systems to determine which one is best to place a particular trade on. You can see them all from your computer screen.

I believe the key is to start with 10 to 15 stocks in order to get a sense of who is controlling and moving them. Start by making small trades until you feel more comfortable. As you get more experienced you can begin to make larger trades. When you begin to grow your portfolio, you can take longer positions (weeks, months, years) where you really look to stabilize your trading activities and use this to hedge your risk. What you will realize then is how many different ways there are to make money in the market.

So why is it that you hear about so many people who are unsuccessful as electronic traders?

It is absolutely crucial to understand that for your first two to six months, you should not expect to make a lot of money. You are just buying time and getting a feel for a particular group of stocks. You really should not expect to be making much money. The way a stock moves during a single day is very different than most people realize. People who come into electronic trading expecting to make a ton of money right away and take 1,000-share positions in stocks don't understand and tend to burn out quickly.

The market is as dangerous as it is rewarding. You must come in realizing this and make smart trades from the beginning. People who start slow and gain experience by making strictly 100-share trades for the first three or four months, expecting losses and no returns, stand to have a much higher success rate over time. When you start understanding your particular stocks better, you can begin making 300- or 400-block trades and then increasing them over time. People who are patient are going to win out over the people who expect too much, too soon.

How would you describe your trading philosophy?

I really focus on things that make sense to me. I follow a set group of Internet stocks, get to learn their personalities and understand how they behave given certain market conditions and news. For example, when the Nasdaq is down 30, 55, or even 70 points, certain stocks tend to get hit harder than others and some tend to bounce more quickly. Remember, one can make money by shorting a stock as it goes down just as easily as buying a stock when it goes up. It's just riskier because a stock can only go down to zero, but it can go up forever. I also look for the big buyers, like institutional brokerage firms and influential market makers; the individuals who make a market in a stock. Market makers are required to keep a trading market active for their particular stock by buying and selling shares from their personal account.

I can name every Internet stock and the two market makers who control that stock. Seeing the way they trade for their own account helps me to gauge the momentum of a particular stock. Take, for example, a situation where the Nasdaq is down 55 points and the two market makers in a couple of the large Internet stocks, Yahoo! and Amazon.com, start to slowly buy the stock back at a slightly higher price. You realize that the stock is about to turn up; it's just a question of how fast you can buy the stock and whether the momentum from the market makers' trades will be enough to get other individuals interested in buying at a higher price as well. Everything happens in a matter of seconds, so you have to be able to act extremely quickly.

What do you mean by understanding the personality of a stock?

To understand the way a stock moves, it helps to create a story for that stock. By understanding how individual pieces of market news affect it and how it normally reacts to information, you can piece together a story and anticipate the stock's movements. The key is to understand the fluctuation levels of a stock price.

In the Internet sector, there can be a lag time with certain stocks. Some days a stock may not move more than a couple of points, even if news is released, and other days it may be up 35 points due to general market sentiment. For example, I was watching Yahoo! recently. It was dormant at 175 when other Internet stocks were just going up like crazy. Then Yahoo! began to tumble and reached 150, at which point I quickly realized it was a great buying opportunity and proceeded to buy shares. In a matter of 45 minutes, it had stormed back up 30 points. I then noticed that Yahoo! was scheduled to release earnings in eight days, so I began to build an even larger position in anticipation that positive earnings would be reported. Last time Yahoo! reported earnings the stock ran up 200 points in five days. So I thought I'd better be ready. Although it did not rise by that much, it did go up 50 points and made me a tidy profit.

By piecing together the story in my mind I created a strategy for myself that helped me think ahead of the masses. We're in a bull market, not a bear market, and Internet stocks are not usually idle for too long before they start to fluctuate up or down. The important questions to ask yourself when creating your story for a particular stock are: Can you remember how a stock behaved at a historic price level? How does your stock react when certain market makers buy and sell it? What happens when your stock gets upgraded by an equity research analyst? Is it a stock that generally opens up and closes down over the course of a trading day? Is it an Internet stock with the possibility of a stock split that will create three or four days of upward momentum? Analyzing this information forces you to interpret market data in ways which will help you understand the way a stock moves over time.

What do you look for in the stocks you trade?

I watch for when my favorite stocks take a real downturn. To me, this represents a great buying opportunity. I say the stock is "on sale." By understanding the movement and history of the stock, I can tell when it has bottomed out and is ready to head back up. Again, I only place trades on stocks that I really understand. Although I may miss out on what is going on in other stocks, I am much more comfortable placing trades on stocks that I follow closely.

How do you handle taking losses?

I never take a position that's bigger than I can handle. I won't ever lose more than a certain predetermined amount I am comfortable with in a day. No matter how convinced I am that a stock will turn around, I will always end my trading day if I am down a certain amount. Fortunately, this does not happen that often, and I have been able to build up my capital base so that I can afford to take some losses. The most important thing is that I have disciplined myself to follow a certain strategy, which mitigates my risk. You just have to realize that sometimes, even if everything is indicating a stock is about to surge up, it can still plummet down. And some days you just have bad luck. It's going to happen. You're going to take losses. The key is to know how much you can lose.

You never want to be in a position where you change your strategy or the fundamentals of what you're doing. This will increase the fear factor. By sticking to a regimented strategy you are in more control of your trades and are able to automatically discipline yourself. Because of the volatility in the markets, I've been down over $20,000 at some point during numerous days; on at least a quarter of those days I've actually finished up over $10,000. As long as you stick to your strategy and discipline yourself, you are able to lessen your risk and take on larger positions when they arise. The key is to always have a sense of where you are on a daily basis. There is more to electronic trading than just the trading part; you have to have a strategy and be able to stick to it, while updating over time.

How has your trading philosophy changed over time?

Originally, my philosophy was very basic: I would be furious if I was in a stock that was up a point and it closed up 3½, but I had sold it when it was only up 2¼. That was an extra $1,000 I could have made! After a while you learn to relax a little bit. If I buy a stock at 30 and it goes up to 35, (where I sell it), and I see indicators once again that the stock may go up even more, I will buy it again. It was much simpler before the rise in Internet stocks, but the rewards were not as good. It's much more difficult now, but the rewards, when you get them, are amazing.

Stocks now trade within 40 point ranges, and if you make a sale three points from the top, you're very happy. The other morning, I had a 4,000-share position in a stock that opened at $79, (where I bought it), went up to $89, down to $74, and then back up to $96 in less than an hour. When electronic trading first began, there was no volatility from Internet stocks and being down $20,000 was a week's worth of work. You had to come back the next day and start steadily building your profits back up. Now, you can recover them in under an hour.

When I started out in electronic trading, I actively traded over 30 stocks. That would be impossible now because of the volatility of individual stocks and the fact that you can trade 100-share increments. Before, you had to trade 1000-share increments. As soon as they changed the rules, all of the electronic traders thought, "Oh well, that's the end of us." We didn't think we were going to be able to get in and out of positions so easily anymore.

But what it did was stretch out the trading ranges of the stocks and increase the opportunity to make even more money. Now the key is not to trade a lot of stocks. You can't do it; you can't follow all of them as closely as you need to. Even a stock such as General Motors, a blue chip stock, usually only moves in a three-point radius over the course of a day. It is extremely difficult to make money off of this stock because if you miss the one big movement for the day, you don't make any money. All I do now is follow a couple of Internet stocks and only place trades on them. Strangely enough, if you are following the right stocks, at least one thing happens every day in each of them that allows you to make money.

When did you realize it was the "right time" to become an electronic trader?

The Internet has been the major catalyst in the advent of electronic trading. When I started, I was jealous of the people who had gotten in ahead of me. I thought that they had gotten in at the right time. And then I realized after a year and a half that people looked at me in the same way. When I started in electronic trading in May of 1996, the people who started just six months later looked at me with envy because they thought I had gotten in at the right time.

But due to the amazing rise of the Internet stocks, now is just as good a time as any to get into electronic trading. The action really lies with the technology and Internet stocks. They are the most volatile and have the capacity to generate the biggest and quickest return for your money. My electronic trading account is simply an Internet account; I never buy stocks in other industries. However, I do hold onto some of my stocks for days, weeks, or even months if I really believe in them. There is more money to be made in the market than ever before. You are missing a golden opportunity if you are not taking part in the Internet revolution by trading these stocks, which are creating the foundation of our economy for the next century. It's almost like being able to go back to when cars were first built and having the chance to invest in all of the original forefathers of the car companies. But the car industry took decades to grow, and the Internet industry has sprung up almost overnight.

What market news and information do you look at?

I find one of the best indicators is news of stock splits. For example, last month I noticed a particular stock that I follow, Exodus, was having a shareholders' meeting in a week to vote on whether to approve a stock split. The board of directors had already approved it, but they were waiting for shareholder approval. Seeing the way Internet stocks have behaved upon declaring stock splits, I knew that I could be looking at a huge gain in the stock. So, at the beginning of the week I started slowly buying the stock and watching it very closely. Over the course of the week you could see that people were anticipating the split would be positive, and the volume of trades drove the stock up over 20 points, even before the board approved the split. When the board did approve it, it shot up another 10 points, but I had already made a huge gain from anticipating the market reaction.

Why doesn't the general public know about electronic trading?

Most people believe it's too good to be true. The media does not usually depict it in the right light. This is partly because when people on CNBC come on and talk about electronic trading, they're really not talking about people who are doing what I'm doing. They're talking about online trading, although someday the line will be blurred because there will be electronic traders trading much the same way as online investors trade. Currently, when you use online investor services, you are actually placing your trades through a third party, and you cannot see important strength indicators such as volume and who the market makers are in the stock. Right now there is a huge difference between online investing and electronic trading. Soon investors will come to realize that it only makes sense to place their trades directly instead of using a third party. In time, almost all investors will be electronic traders of sorts.

How is the information different for online investors?

It is impossible to see what is actually happening to a given stock using current online trading systems. You can only get a quote or check historical information. Electronic traders are able to see every market maker that is buying the stock and gauge the relative strength of the stock by seeing instantaneous quotes and volume figures. Also, electronic traders press a button to enter an order and it happens, no waiting. When you enter an order on any online brokerage service, you have to go in, type in the name of the symbol, type in the number of shares you want and specify whether you want to buy it or sell it from your portfolio...which means clicking and dragging on a lot of boxes and losing precious time when the stock price could be changing. You have to then decide whether you want it in your margin or your cash account, you have to specify if you want it to be a market or a limit order, and if it's a limit order, you then have to determine your highest price. Then you click "send order." It takes about 15 seconds before the system plays your order back to you to verify what you've ordered, and finally, you have to confirm the order. It takes another 15 seconds to get to the trading desk, then it takes another 30 seconds to execute it. Electronic traders can make a trade happen in less than three seconds. The market moves so quickly that even a 20-second difference can easily mean a multiple point swing that you could have capitalized on.

How do you think the advent of electronic trading systems which allow investors to trade over the Internet will change the market?

Over the next two years you will see a huge group of online investors make the jump to electronic trading. New software systems such as TRADESCAPE PRO offered by TRADESCAPE.*com*, will play a huge role in this. People will realize that it is not rocket science to interpret market data and that it is incredibly easy and more efficient to trade directly than by using a third party. There will continue to be skeptics, but there will inevitably be a ton of investors who make the switch, both in the U.S. and eventually overseas. Our markets are naturally heading to a more direct system, and it is only a matter of time before capitalizing on the markets requires a direct trading system.

How do you explain to people what you do? Do people get confused and think you are a stockbroker?

I just tell them I trade stocks, and there's some kind of euphoria that comes along with that now. It's like "Oooh, you trade stocks." Everyone's always loved the stock market. I don't ever say broker, but some people do think I'm one because they don't understand. I have to explain that I trade stocks and shuffle them around, not just invest in them. Although, like I said before, I have altered my trading strategy over time and am in some stocks for longer periods of time now. If someone were to ask me what I do now, I'd tell them I actively trade Internet stocks and then hedge these trades with some long-term positions. It's funny, though, people are so curious about it. The interest in electronic trading is absolutely skyrocketing.

So why isn't everyone becoming an electronic trader?

Probably because of the learning time it takes to become a good trader and the fact that you need some money to get into it.

You've also got to have a logical, sharp, math-oriented mind. In addition, some people are misguided into thinking that electronic trading is too risky. I think a lot of people get discouraged because they come in expecting too much and blow $20,000 to $30,000 in their first month and are out of money. After I gained experience with my $25,000, I actually took out a loan for $100,000 and started leveraging my trades that way. There's no free money out there. There's no blanket of support, either, if you're not trading well. If you're not trading well, you're not making any money. Everything takes hard work. The only way to make good returns is to get your capital base up, and the only way to get your capital base up is to be independently wealthy or learn how to trade well. And the only way to learn how to trade well is by hanging in there; and if you don't have a lot of capital to trade with, it can take up to a year.

What will happen if Internet stocks start to cool down?

The Internet is proof that anything is possible and that an entirely new industry can be born in a matter of a few short years. There is no way to tell what industry may be next, or when it will be, but this is what makes electronic trading exciting. As long as world affairs continue to remain fairly calm, the U.S. will still remain the epicenter for financial activities and money will continue to come pouring in. So I don't know what the next major industry is going to be, but I do know there will be something, and probably a lot sooner than most people would imagine. I like to joke that there will be a laser revolution, whereby lasers will be able to fix emotional problems. My friends all laugh at me, but who would have thought the Internet would have revolutionized our economy in only a few short years? It is just exciting knowing that new things will come along. And you can bet I will be ready for the next one as well.

Do you think the abundance of opportunities to make money will continue for electronic traders?

I really believe that electronic trading opportunities will only continue to grow. The markets are naturally heading towards a system which is more direct, and electronic trading is the logical outcome of that. The only thing that could slow down the incredible intra-day movements of Internet stocks is if the stocks split so many times and have too many shares in the marketplace, which reduces their volatility. America Online can still go up 16 to 18 points on a really good day, but it used to be that it could go up 28 or 32 points. However, the fact that AOL can still go up 16 points in a day, and that some of the other Internet stocks can go up 40 points in a day, tells me one thing: We're still in a bullish market and probably will be for some time to come.

3

ELECTRONIC TRADING STRATEGIES

—Dan Ripoll

D AN RIPOLL LEFT A FINANCE JOB AT MERRILL LYNCH IN 1997, AND WON'T GO BACK. HE HOPES TO BE DAY TRADING FOREVER. DAN BELIEVES THAT ELECTRONIC TRADING IS ALL ABOUT HAVING ACCESS TO THE RIGHT INFORMATION AND THE RIGHT TECHNOLOGY. ADD DISCIPLINE, SPEED, AND A WILLINGNESS TO TAKE LOSSES TO THE MIX, AND YOU'VE GOT THE MAKINGS OF A SUCCESSFUL ELECTRONIC TRADER.

How did you get started in electronic trading?

I started my career as a market maker with Merrill Lynch and I wasn't happy working in a situation where I was constantly the low man on the totem pole. I didn't have any freedom or flexibility to make my own decisions. I left for that specific reason—to be able to make my own call, to be in a place where the money I make is directly related to the decisions I make. In electronic trading, the rewards are instantaneous: you buy the stock and it either goes up or down; you either make or lose the money. There's no bias; there's no one else to consult about making decisions. I started in October of 1997 and want to be doing this forever.

How did you develop your trading strategy?

The first thing I did was really sit back and study particular stocks. I would look for stocks that were strong on a particular day and then follow those stocks the next day to see how they reacted. I found that if something is up three to five points one day, there's a good chance that it may be up again the next day. There is usually some sort of news or other market information that is moving the stock, so I would keep my eye on how the stock continued to react. I began to realize that I was right. I would even go out long on these stocks overnight; they'd go up on the open a lot of times, and I would have made money overnight. The next day, the momentum would continue. People have a habit of always being into something new, so I had the idea that maybe by following through on a set group of stocks I could really excel. Every single person has a different electronic trading strategy. I just found one I was comfortable with, and that worked.

So how long do you typically hold a stock?

It really depends on the situation. I don't really have any rules for that kind of thing. I get in when I feel the stock is going up and then I hold it as long as I think the fundamentals are strong. This can be 10 seconds, an hour, a day, or even longer.

What kind of rules have you made for yourself?

I cut my losses very quickly, and I try not to average down for the day. I have no tolerance for stocks going against me; other traders can accept a loss, and they'll even buy more at the bottom in the belief that it will go up. I have no problem admitting I've made a bad call, but I'd rather lose $1,000 than $10,000. You've got to keep your capital in order to stay alive and in the game. That's my number one rule.

What are the resources necessary to trade successfully?

A good software program that has access to all ECNs and a good back office to make sure trades are cleared. A very important tool can be someone who can make sure that your account balance is what you think it is. You also need access to Island and InstaNet, and you need to make sure they have SOES and SelectNet.

Do you think that the markets in general are heading toward more of a direct model where people place trades directly instead of using a third party, such as a broker, to place the trades for them?

The markets are definitely heading in that direction. People have been getting ripped off for so long by market makers and brokerage firms that they are finally going to realize how easy and more efficient it is to do it on their own. I do think, however, there will always be some kind of market for go-betweens—maybe for large corporations that don't have enough time or are too big and cumbersome to build positions in stocks at good prices. But for small executions, I don't see why it's not better to have direct access to the market yourself. Island is a great example of that: It's so liquid, it's so fast, you never have to wait for an order to get filled, and every order is instantaneous.

What do you see as the difference between online investing and electronic trading?

Electronic trading is execution. Online trading deals with online brokers who cannot give you the speed and the access to the market that electronic traders have. If I see a stock that's about to skyrocket, I can buy 2,000 shares in an instant, whereas online traders have to click in, name a quantity, and so on. While the online trader is pressing enter, I've already made five points. I'm selling it, and he's just getting confirmation of his buy order! He can't see every tick, he can't see who's on the offer, but I can. You're trying to pick off momentum. Let's say that there's a stock that's 56 bid offered at a half. A market maker, say Goldman Sachs, goes high bid at 3/8, Merrill Lynch joins them at 3/8 and there are five people offered at 1/2. If those offers start leaving, someone's paying that offer. You get in and you buy stocks at 3/8 as well so that you can sell them higher. You're detecting momentum, and you're getting in with the buyer. We have access to that—we can see those ticks, we can see those moves. The people using online brokerage firms can't see that.

How would you recommend making the jump from online investing to electronic trading?

If somebody's going to be serious about trading stocks at any level, there is no reason not to use the best tools out there.

This is what electronic trading is all about: having access to the most information and the best technology possible in order to access the markets. You can join an electronic trading firm or use the software to do it out of your own home. The opportunity is there; anyone who wants to do it can do it.

Are there any skills you think online investors have that are transferable to electronic trading?

It depends on what level electronic trader you want to become. If you are using electronic trading to have better access to the markets and get in on stocks at the quoted price—not before they tick up three points because you are using on online brokerage and have to wait for confirmation—then almost all the skills are transferable because you are essentially doing the same thing. However, if you are looking for intra-day swings, electronic trading is really its own animal. The fundamentals and the things that investors look at when buying a stock don't really apply to intra-day swings. It's about recognizing momentum and having a feel for whether or not something is strong.

How important is discipline when you're trading?

I think it's the most important thing. When you start out, you need to be trading in very small increments. No matter what stage you are at in the game, you need to be afraid. People won't say that, but most successful traders fear the market; they fear what could happen to them if they're not disciplined. If you lose that fear and you're careless, you can get caught up in a disaster. If you're careful and you respect the market, then you have a chance to survive and prosper.

**What does it mean to "keep your orders small"—
a couple of hundred shares, a hundred shares?**

That's very subjective, depending on how much capital you
have to trade with. When you're first starting out, maybe
that's 100 shares. You have to experiment and learn without
taking on risk that can really hurt you. When you start getting more comfortable with your trading strategy, then you
should increase your trades.

How do you handle the losses when they come?

It used to bother me a lot when I first started, but now I've
come to terms with it. Everybody's going to have losses. The
difference between the guy who's bothered and the guy who's
not bothered by it is money: if you don't have a lot, then a loss
is a big deal. If you have adequate capital and you don't gamble any more than you can afford to lose, then you're okay. I
look at a loss as a bad day, and that I'm going to make it back
again tomorrow. When you lose and you say to yourself you
have to make it back right now, that's when you get into trouble. Whenever I've had that attitude—let's say I'm down five
points and I'm really down about it—I'll get too aggressive
and take dumb risks and get emotional. The next thing I
know, I'm down 15, wishing I were down five. The difference
is having adequate capital, being confident and knowing
when to cut your losses.

**What are some of the things you look for
in the stocks that you trade?**

I look for a potential big move—I don't want to trade something
that's stagnant. I look for stocks that don't have a huge float—

I want stocks that can move when an order comes in. When I'm right about a stock, I want to see a 5- or 10-point move.

What are the stocks that you trade?

It changes all the time, but usually whatever is hot. I trade only Internet—whatever is moving that day is what I trade. If that changes, then I'll be in whatever group of stocks are moving next.

What makes for a successful electronic trader?

I think being aggressive at the right times, being disciplined, going with your convictions, and being able to admit when you're wrong.

How do the strategies change from trader to trader?

I think it's a reflection of their personalities more than anything else. The amount of risk they take on, the types of stocks they trade, the amount of money they make are all reflective of the traders' personalities.

How do you update your trading strategy over time?

I just get a feel for what's happening, and I talk to people. I'm very observant about what's working and what's not. You'll notice certain stocks or groups of stocks doing certain things and you'll find there are patterns you can follow. You have to talk with other traders and observe the changes in the markets, and then you need to be willing to adjust your strategies. I learned that lesson last winter. January was my best month, and then February was my worst, because the markets changed and I didn't adjust. If you pay attention to little things, little signals, and then you talk about them with other people, you can figure out what's going on and update your strategy accordingly.

What are the different methods traders use to hedge their risk?

I only take on a lot of risk when I know that there's a lot of money to be made in a breakout position. One way to really cut down on risk is not to hold on to any positions over night. If you go out flat at the end of the day and you just trade intra-day, you really cut down on the money that you could lose. The types of stocks that you trade dictate the risk you take on. If you don't have any tolerance for losing money or taking on a lot of risk, you shouldn't get involved in Internet stocks—there's too much volatility. You also want to take into consideration the size of the positions you hold and how much you're willing to let them go down.

How quickly does market news affect a stock, or does it affect it at all for electronic traders?

I think most of the time news is factored in, especially earnings. A lot of the time you'll see a stock selling off on good earnings because it's already gone up 100 points on the knowledge that the earnings were going to be good. I think the real moves come from the momentum of the players getting in or out of the stock.

What sort of technical analysis do you use to help you trade?

I'm a break-out trader, so most of my money is made when stocks break out of a range. So if a stock is in a tight range and it breaks down, I'll make money. Same thing on the long side: if it breaks through a support level, that's also where I make money. That's where the big money is. In a market like this when things are choppy and the stocks are all trading in ranges, I'll look to make money on volatile stocks. When breakouts are happening, I'm much more aggressive and take a lot more risk, as opposed to when the market is quiet.

How have you improved as an electronic trader?

Every day you learn something new and hone your skills a little further. I've tightened my discipline; it is amazing once you start trading your own money how quickly you focus. The fear of losing money really gets you into shape, no matter what level you are at.

What have Internet stocks done for electronic trading?

Internet stocks are the bread and butter of electronic trading right now. That's why people are becoming so interested in electronic trading—Internet stocks swing so wildly that when you're on the right side of the swing, you can make an unbelievable amount of money. When I started electronic trading it was biotech and semiconductor stocks that were hot. There was great money to be made, but stocks didn't go up 50 points in a day—they went up five points, if they were strong. Internet stocks have really gotten people's attention; they've really gotten people's cash registers ringing.

If the Internet went away, would electronic trading still exist?

It would still exist, but it wouldn't be as sexy. People would move onto the next hot group of stocks or some other vehicle to trade that was extremely volatile.

Do you think the market is on the verge of crashing, or are we going to be in a strong market for a while?

I don't think we're going to crash any time soon. Right now we're seeing the distribution of techs and we're seeing money move out of techs into cyclicals. The market's broadening and I think that's healthy. The moves are a little violent and some stocks are oversold, but I think that we're seeing them leveling off to their natural levels.

What do you think will happen to electronic trading if the market crashes?

I think that people who only know how to trade long or don't have any discipline will get wiped out—like Darwinism or natural selection. Good electronic traders who know how to trade long and short and exercise discipline will always be there, and will make money on the market no matter which way it moves.

What are some common misconceptions about electronic trading?

That we don't know what we're doing. That when the market goes down there won't be any money to be made. That we're all sitting at home on an online broker pushing buttons. Electronic trading is an entirely different world. The reports that say most electronic traders lose money are really talking about online traders, because they get horrible executions. They can't help but lose money when they're trading like that. It's like trying to run with a cast on your leg. Electronic trading is direct access to the inside market; it's fast moving, and it's an unbelievable opportunity to make unlimited amounts of money. It's the best thing since sliced bread.

How often do you need to be right in order to make a living and really do well?

If you manage your risk correctly and cut your losses quickly, you can be wrong nearly 60 percent of the time—maybe even more—and still make good money. If you're losing a 1/4 point if you're wrong but making three points when you're right, you're still making a lot of money if you place enough trades.

Do you find that you're always going long on stocks, or do you go short as well?

I do both, but I haven't really gone aggressively short since July or August (1999), when the market was getting crushed every day. It's a lot harder to make money shorting a stock because of the uptake rule: you have to make sure that somebody's willing to buy it there in order to go short. In other words, you can't go short when the momentum is going down;

you have to wait for the momentum to stop going down to go short. That's why it's difficult. When somebody indicates a buy interest, that's usually a signal that it's the bottom of the move. You go short there because you think it's going to go further, whereas a lot of times it won't. If something is going up you can buy it from anybody who's running off the offer; but if it's going down you can't short it unless somebody is willing to pay higher or is willing to pay the offer for it.

Do you find that it helps a lot to be working around other traders?

Actually, I chose the office that I'm in because there aren't a million traders around. I get distracted when I'm in one position and other people are in the opposite position, and they're talking about how I'm long and they're short. I might end up getting out of a position because I was distracted by what the guy next to me was doing. I feel the herd mentality is dangerous. You have to form your own strategy and stick to it until the market changes. I like to let the market dictate your positions, not the person sitting next to you.

What's been the best electronic trading advice you've ever gotten?

Other than being disciplined, the best electronic trading advice that I've ever gotten is "make your play and stay away." It means that when you have a difficult stock that you did well in, don't go back to the scene of the crime and risk losing it.

Do you see yourself doing this for a long time?

I hope I'm doing this forever. It's the best thing I've ever done. No matter how good you are at it, there's always a ton of room to improve. The money's great, but it's not about the money. It's about the challenge of you against the market. When you make the right call, that means you were smarter than all the other people who were out there going against you. It's a thrill.

What do you do when you mentor new traders?

I try to give people a lot of freedom and let them develop their own styles. I don't want them to just mimic my style. Everyone's style should reflect his individual personality. I try to be a guide and to answer questions when they need help, but I don't want to tell them what to do or where to buy or sell. I want them to make those decisions on their own. There's no better lesson than losing money.

How is it possible to come in as a rookie and make money against all these professionals?

I don't think there's any competition specifically between two people. There's enough room for everybody in the market. If you're a quick learner and you're able to exercise discipline, there's no reason you shouldn't be able to come in right away and make money. You just need to get familiar with how stocks move, and if you're a quick study, I think you should be making money within the third or fourth month.

What would be the advice you would give to a novice electronic trader? How long does it take to really learn the ropes?

Everyone's learning curve is different. I caught onto it quick-ly because I had no problem cutting my losses and admitting I was wrong. I think that new electronic traders need to focus and pay attention to what the market is telling you. And don't be afraid to try; don't be afraid to buy something and see what it does. You have to be willing to lose money in order to make money. If you have no tolerance for losing money, this is not the profession for you.

Where do you see the future of electronic trading?

I see it becoming bigger and bigger. Everyone talks about it; everyone wants to do it. People are quitting great jobs in every profession to try their hand at it. We just had corporate bond traders from Salomon and Smith Barney join us. The oppor-tunities are unbelievable. I think a huge appeal is the mobil-ity: you can set up shop anywhere and trade from your com-puter. I'll buy a one-way ticket to Miami knowing that I don't have to come back until I feel like it. There's no one to answer to—you'll work just as hard anywhere you go, and there's enough money to be made in electronic trading that you don't have to be great at it to make a comfortable living. There are people who I don't consider to be good traders at all who are still making six figures and maintaining complete autonomy.

MAKING THE JUMP FROM ONLINE INVESTING

—John Moore and Art Herman

JOHN MOORE AND ART HERMAN BEGAN TRADING IN VERY DIFFERENT WAYS. ART STARTED WITH ONE OF THE FIRST ELECTRONIC TRADING FIRMS IN 1995, AND WAS GIVEN A LARGE AMOUNT OF MONEY TO PLAY WITH. JOHN, IN CONTRAST, STAKED HIS OWN CAPITAL AND RECEIVED NO TRAINING. BUT BOTH SAY THAT DIS- CIPLINE AND STICKING TO YOUR PERSONAL TRADING STRATEGY, NO MATTER WHAT HAPPENS, IS THE KEY TO MAKING IT BIG AS AN ELECTRONIC TRADER.

Explain the difference between online investors and electronic traders.

John: Online investors are like stock speculators. They buy and sell stocks for bigger reasons than an electronic trader does. They might get a tip, or notice something on a chart or find out about a new company from their own research or expe- rience. Their experience with the market would be one of building positions and averaging in—tactics to establish longer-term positions. Longer-term would be a week or weeks at a time, or even longer depending on the investor. What electronic traders do is really trading: we buy on support, sell on resistance, and try to play stocks in a much simpler way. I think you can trade a stock better when you're watching the behavior of the market makers and the behavior of the market, and you accumulate and sell based solely on what you see other traders doing, rather than going on the fundamentals.

Electronic traders essentially trade on the information that the market is giving them. We can see that a bunch of people are buying a stock, the stock is behaving, and we'll be able to capitalize on shorter-term movements. They're doing the research, but we're executing orders based on what we see happening—as it happens. We're able to get out of stocks faster and cleaner and we're not attached to positions. If a stock starts behaving poorly, we don't feel the need to stick around.

How would you recommend that an online investor build the necessary electronic trading skill set?

John: I would say start small. Take what you already know about the market and try to apply it in short-term circumstances. Know that it takes time to make the adjustment, so start small and have patience; give yourself time to learn it. If you're really a big online investor and you trade a few thousand-share lots and you're making good money every month, you can expect that when you make the transition you're going to have to down-size, or otherwise take some losses. The best thing you can do is just watch what's going on.

Should you watch a smaller group of stocks?

John: Yes, one or two at a time. Find whatever is most volatile that day, and watch and trade only those stocks.

What are the resources you need for electronic trading and how are they different from those that you'd use for online investing?

Art: They're totally different. Electronic traders use Nasdaq Level-2 screens and online investors only see the real-time quotes, at best. An electronic trader makes a momentum play, using the Level-2 screens to react to market maker movements. The amount of information per stock is much greater on a Level-2 screen, and you can really only gain access to a Level-2 screen by using electronic trading technology.

So what does a Level-2 screen show you?

Art: A Level-2 screen lets you see not only the inside quote, but the underlying bids and offers as well. We can predict when the momentum will turn by gauging the strengths of the underlying bids and offers. There's a lot more information to really make an educated trade with.

John: The greatest advantage we have is that we can see who's doing what in the market. We can see, for example, that in a certain stock that's going up, one guy in particular is on the bid all day. You'll never see that at home; you might see the stock going up, but you'll have no background as to why. When we're watching that same stock here, instead of just seeing that stock go up, we'll know who's pushing it there. We'll know that when that trader leaves, it's probably going to go down. The online investor at home has no idea and might just think it's another pull-back.

Why do you think the public confuses online investing and electronic trading so much?

John: The media makes no distinction. If you watch CNBC, you'll see that they never note the difference. They'll report something like, "Electronic traders own 60 percent of Lycos," and the fact is, if you're like most day traders trading for the short term, you don't own any Lycos. Not long enough for anyone to measure what you're in, anyway. You may own a couple thousand shares for three or four minutes, but you'll almost always go out flat at the end of the day.

Art: I think the media is three steps behind, because it doesn't seem to me that they understand what it is we do. This is such a new field that I don't think people really have had time to learn about it, and that's why they can't make the distinction.

What do you think are some of the misunderstandings that people have about electronic traders?

Art: We get accused of falsely inflating stocks, when what we really do is improve market depth, liquidity, and pricing efficiency.

Why do people think that you're bad for the market?

John: It's an impossible argument to make—that we're bad for the market. The more shares of a stock that are traded, the truer a price will be. The price of a stock is the number of buyers versus the number of sellers, so in theory, it's always moving to the point where that number is equal and the price will even out. Essentially, the more shares that are traded, the more accurate that price will be. Not to mention that the more shares traded, the narrower the spread becomes.

A few years ago, when electronic trading was just getting started, stock spreads were usually a quarter to as much as two points wide. What that means is that if you're pointing and clicking at home, like online investors, and you want to buy a stock, you'll have to pay 52; if the spread is a point, and you then want to sell your stock, you have to sell it at 51. So there's a dollar difference per share that you sell, and the market maker just pocketed that extra dollar. That's why all those big houses exist, and why they'd created such a monopoly on the market. Now, the more stocks that get traded, the price becomes more accurate and the spread gets thinner. Anyone who's informed on what electronic traders do can't make the argument that electronic traders are bad for the market, because what we really do is provide efficiency and equality in investing.

What about people who say that electronic trading is too risky?

John: It is risky, but that's not a fault. People just need to know what they're getting into before they try their hands at electronic trading. You need to start out small and be prepared to lose money in the beginning—everybody does. It's a big, high-speed, high-stakes poker game and there's no way you can win without sitting down at the machine and learning the game. The upside is that it's also very lucrative; once you've put your time in, you'll make more money with less risk doing this than through speculating or online investing.

Do you think we're moving more toward a market where online investors are going to make the jump to electronic trading?

John: If they're serious about making money in this business, electronic trading is the best spot to be.

Art: Right now online traders are trading with one arm tied behind their backs. They could be using Nasdaq Level-II screens, trading with professional information—the same information that market makers have. Instead, online investors are rallying their orders through a big, slow, bureaucratic mess. If people want to do this seriously, making the jump to electronic trading is in their best interest.

What impact has the increased number of people actively trading stocks had on the market?

John: The more people trading stocks, the better and more accurate the market is.

Art: One way that electronic trading has changed the face of investing is that stocks react more quickly to news and information than they did a few years ago. Basically, there are more people entering the market who are enabling investors to have more control over their money. I agree with John that the markets are becoming more efficient. Traders who are good will increase their capital more quickly, and be able to leverage it into even greater returns.

Where do you see the field of electronic trading heading?

John: Ever since day one, there have been naysayers, people saying that electronic trading is a dead-end field, and all that ever happens is that the market keeps changing and we keep making money because we have the best tools to access the markets. Today, you might make money with one strategy, but next year you'll be doing something different.

Art: Trading has been around for hundreds of years. It's not going anywhere. It's just going to get better. One effect that technology's had on the market is that stocks move faster; when a stock takes a dive, it can take only one day, whereas a few years ago it might have taken three months. Same thing with the Internet stocks: it might have taken years for stocks to run up like that. Now it's faster because of technology. There are still really good opportunities down the road for electronic traders. Your job is to sit and look at the prices of stocks as they move, and you make more money the faster the prices change. And it's only going to get faster.

Why is it that right now, most electronic traders are actively trading only technology and Internet stocks?

John: The only reason we're biased that way is because we trade only Nasdaq stocks. We would really trade anything that's hot on any given day. A year and a half ago, we were trading semiconductors; earlier this year, a lot of people made money on biotechs. It seems like electronic trading is very Internet-focused, but the truth is that we have the power to transfer all our power and attention to whatever is happening that day. People talk about beating the S&P. Imagine that every day of the year, you own the best S&P stock. Your percent gain would be through the roof. In the ideal electronic trading world, you're devoting 100 percent of your capital and attention to whatever's hot that day.

Do you think that the markets in general are heading toward a direct trading approach?

John: They almost have to, because it's a better way to trade stocks. As much as the people who have monopolies on the markets will kick and scream, they can't deny that it's a better way to trade.

Art: You can't really fight it at this point. It has already gone too far towards a direct model with advances made in technology.

How did you first develop an electronic trading strategy, and what did you find useful?

Art: My advice for newcomers would be to look at how much money you have and then determine how much you can afford to gamble.

John: What I was told was that before I started trading, I should decide how much I was willing to lose, write it down on a piece of paper, and if I ever hit that number, cash out. People can get obsessive and drive themselves into the ground. I've heard horror stories about losing mortgages. You feel sorry for those people, but you have to think that they need to be a little bit more prudent.

Art: It's also better to be young, because you have less to lose and you can afford to take the risk. This is a professional game: You need to be using the technology of the right electronic trading firm and the best resources. It's like a professional sports team, where you need a good team, a good trainer, and the right equipment to be the most successful.

John: I sat around for a year trading small lots of stock and watching tape, and I basically broke even my first eight months. It took a very long time and I had a low tolerance for risk. Go where it's hot, even if it's a little painful to take the risk.

How can the newcomers compete with people like you who have been in it for a couple of years now?

Art: If they're jumping in with their own money, they better have a mentor looking out for them. We know the rules of the game, we know the ins and outs, and we're faster on the keyboard.

John: But by the same token, we know two guys who just started three months ago who are both profitable now, because they were both well trained. If you want to do this, it's in your best interest to go to a good firm, sit next to a good trader, and ask lots of questions.

What are some of the trading rules that you both live by?

Art: The most important things for any trader to have are discipline and focus. You can't succeed without them.

John: Don't have preconceived notions about what a stock's going to do, and don't get emotional. Be able to get out of a stock if you see it's going down, and don't wait around—react.

Art: If you buy a stock hoping that it will go up and it starts to go down, sell it. If you really still believe it will go up, then you can look to buy it back even cheaper. But everyone has a different strategy, and you need to find the one that works for you. And once you find it, stick to it and don't be tempted to veer away from it in the heat of the moment. Stay disciplined. If you buy stock for a reason and the reason no longer exists and it starts to go down, get out.

John: You can't get emotional about stocks. People loose $500 and they think, "There goes my car payment," but you've got to distance yourself from the money. The more experience you have and the more money you make, the easier it is to remain focused and digest losses and be rational. It's all about surviving the learning curve, because once you hit your first big day, it's all uphill from there.

So do you think people can trade part-time?

Art: If they want to be successful, they have to devote themselves to electronic trading as a career. Every time I try to slack off, just come in for a few hours a few days a week, I get killed.

Is that because you lose touch with the psychology of the market?

Art: Yes. It would be like trying to play with a professional baseball team without coming to spring training and showing up midseason for a game.

So how do you update your trading strategy over time?

Art: You just react to what makes you money. I used to be someone who would buy and hold, I'd go out with 70 positions a night, and that's how I made money for two and a half years. Now I go out flat every night and trade on volatility. Why? Because buying and holding wouldn't work this year.

So do you feel like you're consistently getting better as electronic traders?

Art: I don't know if I'm getting better, but I am making more money every year. Does that mean that I'm a better trader, or does that just mean that the market is going through the roof? I don't know. Maybe the market's getting better, maybe the technology's getting better. I'm adapting, I'm making money, so I'm happy.

John: One thing that will always make you better is keeping your cool and building your confidence. Those two things will help you make clean trades, which will in turn make you more money. It's a cycle that feeds on itself: the more experience you have, the better you get, and the more things that will be tipped in your favor.

Art: Electronic trading is the best opportunity I've ever had, and I've made more money than I ever thought was possible in this amount of time, but it also comes with great risk. You have to take it very seriously. You need to seek training, and you need to have the right equipment—the right software, the right firm, the right capital.

So how long will you do this for?

John: It is my career for right now, but not my career for the rest of my life. I hope one day I'll be able to do speculating a little bit more, where I can sit on the sidelines and watch, because this takes a lot of energy.

Art: I don't know. Right now the opportunities are great and we're having fun.

REALISTIC EXPECTATIONS

—Michael Trica

MICHAEL TRICA IS ONE OF THE CAUTIONARY VOICES IN THE ELECTRONIC TRADING FIELD. HE WARNS THAT AT SOME POINT, THE INTERNET FRENZY WILL COME TO AN END, AND STOCKS WILL FALL TO THEIR TRUE VALUE. HOW TO KEEP WINNING WHEN THE CRAZE COOLS DOWN? REALIZE THAT THE MARKET IS ALWAYS CHANGING AND UPDATE YOUR TRADING STRATEGY ACCORDINGLY, AND DEVELOP THE ABILITY TO ABSORB AND REMEMBER KEY PIECES OF INFORMATION.

What were your first impressions of electronic trading?

Electronic trading has completely changed, even over the last year and a half. It's different in terms of both the players in the marketplace and how the game is played. Electronic trading is much more competitive now. A year and a half ago, it was primarily a question of discipline, knowing the rules of the game, playing by the rules every day and following the law of percentages. By just following those rules, you could not only make a living, but be extremely successful. There are many more variables now.

How do you think electronic traders have affected the state of the markets today?

The way stocks were traded in the past was very institutionally driven. But now individuals control the prices of stocks; individual electronic traders and online investors hold the majority of shares in Internet stocks. I truly feel that the analysts in investment banks know that Internet stocks are overvalued, but no one wants to have the responsibility of driving these stocks down to their correct value. It's in no one's best interest. Everyone's happy if the stocks continue to go up. If they were to drop to where they were supposed to be, institutions and brokerage firms would stand to lose billions of dollars.

What are some of the trading rules that you live by?

I'll never make a trade unless I know what the worst-case scenario is for that given day. I want to understand the news and the earnings forecasts surrounding the stock, as well as where it was a week ago and a year ago. I think it's very important to understand the fundamentals of a stock and not just buy and sell based on momentum.

How is it possible to get all that information and still react quickly enough?

One of the most important things about electronic trading is being able to absorb lots of information and being able to recall that information in an instant. I don't need to refresh my memory every time I see an interesting stock. I already know all the information I need to be able to trade that stock. I know where the stock price has been over the past year and what has effected its movement. Memory and focus are absolutely key.

What have Internet stocks done to the market?

What happens with the game today is that momentum will drive stocks up to several times their actual value, and then it will, in a sense, die. At that point, electronic traders will get out of that stock. So an Internet stock could rise from 10 to 100, with electronic traders involved all the way, but once it starts dropping, electronic traders will evacuate that stock before it hits 90. Then the stock will drift down from 90 to its fair value, which may be 20, but in that drop there won't be any electronic traders involved. So this is how these stocks can drift back down: electronic traders won't get involved because there's no momentum, hence the lack of confidence that if a trader buys it *now*, there won't be someone to buy it at a higher price. It's very similar to a period scheme: everyone is very comfortable paying up for these stocks, even though they know they're overvalued. They know there will be market and liquidity enough to take the stock out at a higher price, and that's why these stocks continue to go up. It's just a game without any fundamentals. Electronic traders are very cognizant of the point at which they need to get out.

How much of an effect has the media had in hyping up particular stocks?

I think the media actually has an amazing power over the price of a stock. It's astounding how one comment in the Wall Street Journal or on CNBC can greatly impact the momentum of a stock. Every day there are examples of stock skyrocketing to 50 percent over it's current value because it's been mentioned in a news segment that day. The profession started out very small in terms of the trader's confidence that momentum and liquidity would allow him to sell a stock at a higher price. It's snowballed into such a phenomenon that one piece of news can drive an Internet stock 10 to 20 points higher. Everyone's so confident that there will be a buyer at a ridiculous price, no one has a problem buying it.

What effect will Internet stocks have on the market in the future?

My personal opinion is that the Internet frenzy eventually has to come to an end. It's either going to be earnings, or it's going to be a change in the general market euphoria concerning anything related to the Internet. One thing or another is going to turn momentum into a lack of liquidity, and people are going to lose the confidence that they can always sell their stock at such a high price. One day, the snowball is going to reverse itself and Internet stocks will take a dive. But electronic traders will be out more quickly than anyone else and moving onto the next thing.

What do you think the general public needs to understand about electronic trading?

There are a lot of opportunities, but it's very important to understand that the market is in a constant state of change, and you have to be able to update your strategy on a second's notice.

What are some of the key traits of successful electronic traders?

Competitiveness is important, and understanding that complacency is not acceptable. Many traders limit their upsides by being complacent, which in turn limits absorption of their trading savvy. Focus is also very important. Traders need to be able to concentrate 100 percent when they are trading, and should be constantly listening and learning to all that goes on around them.

What is it that you enjoy about electronic trading?

The hours are incredible, six and a half hours a day. And I like to know that at the end of the day, I'm not just receiving a check for a certain amount. I'm in control of what it is that I gain or lose. It's a lot of fun.

Should electronic traders set limits on how much money they'll invest?

Electronic traders don't set limits on how low they will let their investments sink as much as online investors do. Because electronic traders have direct access to their accounts, it's easier for them to get in and out of stocks. Some traders do set limits, but more frequently they'll set limits on overall losses for the day. I don't think that's necessarily a good strategy because I feel there have been many times when, if I had set downside limitations, I would have hit them. If you have the confidence to believe in every trade you make, and to know that you'll be able to make money in the end, you will end up with a profit. Trading is not just a purchase and a sale; it's a continual updating of the information that you have access to. Limitations are good for people who have little experience, but for the more experienced electronic trader, limitations could actually hurt you.

How do fundamental changes in the market as a whole affect your trading strategy?

They really force you to keep the pulse of the market and continually update your trading strategy. This is why the "old school" electronic traders have been so successful. They have seen the ups and downs of the market and understand the way particular stocks react. You are absorbing new pieces of information every day that give you a better insight into the personalities of stocks.

How confident are you when you make a trade?

Confident enough that I won't make the trade unless I truly believe that it is going to work out. I'll get involved in a lot of different types of stocks on a limited scale, so that I have a scenario where if the market goes up, I'll make money, and if it goes down, I'll make money. In order to do that, you really need to be both long in a stock (for when it goes up) and short in a stock (for when it goes down). It's just a matter of how quick and decisive you are, and how intuitive you are about forecasting what the stocks are going to do.

What types of people are getting into electronic trading now?

A lot of new people are getting involved, but the profession has changed so much. There's been a definite growth in the sheer number of electronic traders out there, and the fundamentals have really changed. It's all because of the Internet. The main focus for electronic traders right now is Internet stocks. And Internet stocks are very momentum-based with no fundamentals backing them. You must constantly be updating your strategy and really be in touch with the market and the particular stocks you trade.

How is it possible for these new groups of people getting into electronic trading to compete with the professionals?

Anyone who wants to try his hand at this field needs to invest many, many months learning how to trade. I really feel that you need to get yourself involved in a firm with lots of professional traders who have a lot of experience. And there are companies out there that are more than willing to invest time in individuals who are willing to learn the profession. Like any other career, it's just a matter of time until you have that experience.

What would you suggest as the first step to get a feel for electronic trading?

The first step, and it's an easy step, is to turn on CNBC and just watch it to get a feel for the action of the market. At first, it might not make any sense to you, but eventually you'll learn more and more about what is actually happening. Also, read the newspaper; the Wall Street Journal is a great place to start. However, the best thing is to engage actual traders in conversations so you can get a feel for the psychology of electronic trading.

What advice would you give to people who are committed to becoming electronic traders?

Invest time and capital to learn the fundamentals of electronic trading and don't assume any earning potential for at least a year. The investment of time is the most crucial at the beginning. I think people tend to jump in thinking that electronic trading is so easy and that everyone wins. That's probably because you always hear from people when they are doing well, but you don't really hear about it when they lose. A new trader looking to establish a career in electronic trading has to invest a lot of time and limit capital expenditure. It can be very risky, especially at the beginning when you're learning. Some electronic trading firms have what is called a "trading module," where you are trading, but it's all fantasy. You're on the same system, you're bidding and offering stocks, you're looking at the same tools that the other traders are using, but none of your executions are real. This is really a great way to get started, because you can practice for a month or so before you actually start trading for real.

How important is it to have a large amount of money to trade with?

I think it is very important. And there are ways to leverage it if you don't. Most institutions and some electronic trading firms are willing to lend money depending on the rate of return. In many places, margin rates go as low as 10 to 15 percent. When the prospects are a chance to earn 100 percent on a given day, on that money, it's a great opportunity. Increasing numbers of lenders will enter the marketplace as a way to make much higher returns by lending money to electronic traders while the market is strong.

What is it that the average electronic trader does wrong?

If a given electronic trader has the knowledge and experience that comes from investing the time to learn the game, he really can't go wrong. It's all about understanding the market mentality. Once you know how to trade, it's all a matter of mentality, focus, and an understanding of risk and reward. So you really can't make a bad trade. You can lose your focus; you can lose your perspective on risk and reward and worst-case scenarios, but it's all a matter of buying and selling and picking your prices.

What are some of the physical tools you need for electronic trading?

It's very important that you have a news service. And, although it seems basic, what's also a very important piece of equipment is a TV, so that you can listen to CNBC all day. It's great ambient noise because it broadcasts the moment-to-moment feel of the market. It is also extremely important to have a top-notch computer with high-speed lines to the Internet. Last but not least, I think it's great to have other experienced traders around you. I learn so much just by sitting near people who have been trading for more years than I.

What are the things to look for at the different electronic trading firms out there?

The first thing you want is to make sure that your firm has the most up-to-date tools for electronic trading. Proprietary technology to access Level-I and Level-II quotes is not the same at every firm. Different electronic trading systems allow you to bid and offer in different ways and each one has its own distinct feel.

What is the most important thing to look for?

The speed of access is very essential. An electronic trader should not be trading on anything with direct access less than a T1 Internet line. An electronic trader should not be trading on a conventional modem because it's too slow, and that split-second is going to make all the difference. You also really want to look for an electronic trading firm that has electronic traders who are doing extremely well. At the top-notch firms, there's competition to sit next to the best traders because you learn so much watching them and listening to them all day.

How are the strategies used by online investors different from those used by electronic traders?

Online investing is totally different from electronic trading. In electronic trading, you need to have two different understandings: First, what is your worst-case scenario for a specific stock you are buying or shorting, and second, knowing at what point to exit your position. When I make a trade, I have to know what my risk and reward scenarios are. If I buy a stock right here, right now, given the fundamental underpinnings of the stock and the market at the present moment, what is the worst thing that could happen? That's a more difficult scenario than trades made by online investors because they are used to buying for the future, and if something goes bad for them that day, they can still hold on to the stock and realize a profit further down the line. The worst case scenario is different for a long-term position than it is for a very short-term position.

What skills are transferable from online investing to electronic trading?

I think that a basic fundamental understanding of stocks and their price histories, as well as the technical information that accompanies that knowledge, are important for any form of trading or investing.

Is there any way you could become a day trader on a part-time basis?

You could do it part-time, but even when I go away for a week I feel really out of touch with the market perspective when I return. Being there part-time greatly limits your profit potential. Of course, you can do it as many hours a day as you like, but the more you do it, the more confidence you'll have in what you're doing and the more conviction you'll have when you make a trade and the greater your success rate will be.

If you could say one thing to people interested in electronic trading, what would it be?

You cannot be a day trader if you're faint of heart. You have to have the ability to go home at the end of the day and not necessarily be in a better position than you were in at the beginning of the day. You need to have the perspective that some days you're going to lose money, some days you're going to make money, but if you follow the rules that you've set for yourself, everything will work out in the end.

How long do you plan on continuing to day trade?

I enjoy it so much that I don't really see myself doing anything else. I look forward to doing it for as long as it's possible and profitable.

Where do you see the future of electronic trading ?

Where electronic trading is right now is just the beginning. Electronic trading is a phenomenon that has come about as a result of technological advances and direct access to the markets. Electronic trading is just going to grow: individual investors will be able to make use of the ability to directly buy and sell stocks through very fast, convenient, and reliable sources that make it a more efficient way to trade or invest.

Do you think that the direct aspect of electronic trading is the prototype for markets in the future?

Definitely. With the announcement of the extension of hours on the NASDAQ as well as on the NYSE, it will definitely be easier, cheaper, and more reliable for individual investors to get the price that they want, and liquidity will probably be increased based on that. Individuals who learn the electronic trading skills now are putting themselves in a great position for the future. Just wait and see.

6

PUTTING THE ODDS IN YOUR FAVOR

—Jonathan Tanzman

Focus. Be patient. Don't be scared to take a loss. Above all, protect your downside. These are the strategies that John Tazman uses day in and day out. By combining these techniques with constant vigilance for market indicators that put the odds in his favor, his net result is usually the same: extremely positive.

How have you become a successful electronic trader?

I approach electronic trading by looking at the things that can hurt you and make you lose. When you have a profession where the odds can routinely go in your favor by being patient and disciplined, the only way you are going to lose is by being careless. I have always recognized from working with other electronic traders, and from my own experience, that the kind of mistakes most people make could be avoided by just being patient. Probably 30 percent of the time, people buy stock out of frustration or boredom because they have not been active for 45 minutes or they are a little bit restless. You should only buy a stock when the market is strong and market conditions are favorable. Nonetheless, many electronic traders end up buying stock when they should not—like when they're eating lunch at their desk, and they see something move on their screen and buy, even though they are not focused on what is going on. Also, many beginning electronic traders will get a lot more aggressive and try to recover if they are having a bad day, without paying attention to overall market conditions. After six years of electronic trading, I have become successful because I stick to my strategy and I am a patient and disciplined electronic trader.

How do you decide which stocks to trade?

It changes over time, but fundamentally, I prefer a stock that does not tick all day. I will stay away from stocks like Dell or Amazon because their prices move continuously, giving market makers the reason to continuously adjust their positions. Therefore, I trade what I refer to as "third level stocks" that have two- to three-point ranges all day. When they move, there is generally something more behind it. I have a group of stocks that over time has been cut down a third based on the fact that moves are a lot bigger than they used to be. I have narrowed my scope so the ones that I do play, I can watch closely over the day and not miss a downturn that could cost me two to three points.

**How many stocks do you follow
during a given day?**

You always have to update and change your strategy because the market is in a continuous state of change. I went from going out with 20 to 30 positions every night, to always going out flat, because the market is now so volatile that you do not need to take the extra risk of holding the positions overnight. Now I have a group of about 50 "third level stocks," so I am not overloaded with information, and I can pretty much follow everything that is going on with these stocks over the course of a day. At the same time, I try to pick up a stock that comes into play that I have not watched for a while and re-initiate my coverage on it. I am really always watching for the one or two of my stocks that are in play for that particular day.

What are some of the fundamental and technical analyses you use to monitor your positions?

There is very little on the technical side. I don't use charts and I don't research companies very much. Whereas, in the past I would have said you do not need to understand charts, now I think it is a definite advantage to have that knowledge. I have spent so much time looking at market maker behavior and market maker positioning that all the clues that traders pick up from looking at technical analyses I pick up from watching market makers. When I see Goldman Sachs selling at a particular price, I may not know their true intentions, but I remember their previous activity in the stock and have some idea of where the price is heading. By understanding market maker movements and remembering which market maker is buying where, and at what price, I am able to judge where the stock price is heading. My approach is just another way of interpreting market data.

How do you understand the movements of market makers?

The number of market makers in NASDAQ stocks has greatly increased over the last couple of years. You really have to pay attention to all of the market makers in the particular stocks you follow and learn the movements and previous activity within that stock. One of the first tricks I learned is that the market makers you have to pay the most attention to are the ones that are the last to leave a level. When you see a pattern developing within a stock that gets disrupted, you have to take very careful notice of the market maker that breaks the pattern and watch its movements. The most successful electronic traders are the ones who can anticipate the effect their activity will have on the market on a consistent basis. This only comes from watching market maker activity within a stock for some time.

What are some of the ways you hedge your risk?

One of the things I have learned from teaching people is that although everyone understands the importance of risk/reward, not many people really understand what the risk is when they take a position. Many new traders get in trouble because they do not understand the combined effects of market makers, ECNs, and other electronic traders, and do not realize the full downside risk on a given position. However, when I get into a stock I know exactly what my downside risk is, and I am extremely disciplined about getting out of it if it reaches that point. Some people will not get out if they see strong market makers such as Goldman Sachs trying to push the stock back in their favor. This can be a recipe for disaster. You always have to have a risk/reward strategy and stick to it religiously. You also have to be aware, in more volatile stocks such as Yahoo!, that you could surrender a one-point loss very quickly before you are able to get out. If you are careful and disciplined, you can go months at a time getting out of positions at your set level.

What are the first things you teach a new electronic trader?

The first and most important lesson is protecting your down-side. As time goes by you do not want to be afraid of losses. The person who is going to make the most money is going to lose money at some point as well. You want to care about every level a stock moves—1/16, 1/8, 1/4. When you get involved in a stock and it does not work out, be careful. Be disciplined. Second, newer traders need to be extremely patient. When the market is hot, you see a lot of people around you active in the market, and there is a tendency to compromise and try to jump in as well. Again, be patient. There are a lot of experienced electronic traders in the market now, and you need to buy and sell when the opportunities match your pre-determined criteria, not just because you are anxious to start trading.

How long does it take to get started in electronic trading?

It depends on how much you want to be involved. If you want to make day trading your career you need to devote three to six months of full-time study of the markets and other electronic traders. Experienced day traders have the opportunity to go out in any market and make a very nice living.

What is the right amount of capital to get started with?

It really depends on each individual and his risk/reward comfort level. If you are going to be among the most successful traders you are going to have to be able to buy $500,000 worth of stock; however, with $35,000 to $50,000 of your own money, you can still make quite a bit of money. That does not mean that if you have saved $80,000 over your whole life you should go and day trade with all of that money. Only trade with money you can afford to lose.

What is it you need to look for in electronic trading tools?

You really need a hardware system that is reliable and does not go down. You need an environment where people are making money and credit a lot of it to the software and system they are using. Each electronic trader has different tools he likes to use, but when you are starting, you should have all the basics, from charts to tickers.

What do you see as the most common reason people are not successful as electronic traders?

The main reason electronic traders do not make it is difficulty coping with loss or pressure situations. People who cannot stand to take a loss from time to time or lose their confidence, are not cut out for this business. Once a person loses confidence, he might as well move on, because you have to have the courage to take on, aggresively, some level of risk. In addition, a lot of people have trouble concentrating for a six-plus-hour day. This may not sound like a long period of time; however, you have to be intensely focused for all 6-plus hours, and it is extremely draining.

How do new electronic traders avoid getting exploited by the experienced traders?

The best way is to find a mentor who will teach you the basics. There are a lot of one-week programs out there that will help you get started, but they will not make you a great electronic trader. You have to find a person who is willing to show you the ropes and really care, even if you have to give him a cut of your winnings. However, this is not to say that you may not be better than he is even after six months.

Anyone coming in should have the confidence that he can be the best.

Have you become more confident in your trading skills over time?

For a long time I have felt that I should make money every day. I have certain things that work for me that have consistently made me money, even though the market keeps changing. The key is to update your strategy continually, and to be confident of your ability to make money and capitalize on all of the opportunities that present themselves in the marketplace.

Do you do anything in the morning to get prepared for the day?

Anyone who walks in at 9:00 or 9:15 to trade the market will not be ready. I think you need to get in at least an hour early to get ready, read the paper, and, especially, to monitor your positions from the previous day. Go over each trade from the day before and analyze why you made the trade, what the market conditions were, and whether you made the sale at the appropriate time. If you go through your own reports very carefully, you will be able to analyze your trading style and be much more prepared for the trading day.

How different is the strategy of each electronic trader?

Traders who are the most risk averse will buy a stock like Oracle, which has a lot of market makers and a lot of activity, because when you want to get out of a position you can usually limit yourself to a 1/16 point loss. Other traders want to go for bigger positions and simply look at volatility. They get involved with stocks like Yahoo! and Amazon because they will move 20 to 40 points over the course of a day.

Is it possible to control your risk through the particular stocks you trade?

It is definitely possible; however, you have to be careful not to control it to a point where you do not allow yourself the opportunity to make money. You have to decide when you start trading what you are looking to do. Are you looking to dabble in day trading for fun and maybe make $50,000 a year, or are you looking trade aggressively and make millions?

What effect will online investing have on electronic trading?

There is a large overlap between the two. You have a large group of people who now look at the markets every day and really enjoy it and want to take the leap to experiment with electronic trading. I think people will be surprised at how many of them actually take the jump.

Would you say electronic trading is a lot riskier than online investing?

If you are using risk capital, they both carry the same weight. You can be an electronic trader and risk too much and an online investor and risk too much. Neither one, by nature, is flat-out risk. The risk is what you can afford to lose in terms of time and opportunity.

What effect will electronic trading software that allows online users to access electronic trading tools have on the market?

Although your guidance level is much lower because you are not in the electronic trading atmosphere, you can still get a feeling for it online. Then, if you decide to get more serious about it or want to do it full-time, you can join an actual electronic trading firm. Every city around this country will eventually have 15,000 to 50,000 people who are going to be electronic trading on some level, and Internet access will definitely play a major role. Companies such as TRADESCAPE.*com* are already offering it online.

What created this opportunity for electronic traders?

For many years, the markets were really only accessible to Wall Street insiders. Any logical inroads by other groups, and, especially, the general public, were greeted with a lot of resistance. The SEC began realizing this and gradually changed the rules to make access to the markets more feasible for others. Once it was clear that the electronic traders were directly aligned with the public in general, the SEC started supporting the electronic traders as well.

What do you see as the role of the SEC now?

We are at a point where electronic trading is an accepted part of the industry. Long before I got in the markets, there was a lot of fraud and some shady firms that did not give people the support they needed, which created a somewhat tainted name for day trading. However, as years have gone by these firms have been weeded out, and a lot better options, which the SEC supports, exist for electronic traders.

What kind of effect would a market crash have on day trading?

The crash itself would not end day trading as we know it. The aftereffects could really hurt it. Even if the Dow dropped to 7000, the biggest problem would be if people stopped trading and putting more money in the market. Electronic traders can actually get out of positions more quickly than almost anyone can, so they would stand to lose the least from the crash itself. The big question for day traders is how much activity would be at the new levels. But in my opinion we are still a long way away from this. We have really only had one great year for Internet stocks, and everyone is still waiting to see what happens next. The outlook long-term is still overwhelmingly positive. When the market is going up, there is a lot of extra money entering the market, which means there is a lot of extra money to make all around. So many new people are getting into the business that the volatility and liquidity will still be there for quite some time, even if the market does slow down.

How long will Internet stocks play a large part in the success of day traders?

Internet stocks will be a major force until they crash and burn. This is highly unlikely for a long time or at least until it becomes a sensible playing field where you have certain companies who have built a solid reputation and track record for success and are part of the fabric of this society. There will definitely be stocks that look great today but will be long gone in a number of years. Once those shake-ups happen, the Internet sector may not be the place for day traders to gear themselves to. But this is a long way down the road, and then there will undoubtedly be other opportunities as well.

Why is it that electronic traders look to the NASDAQ instead of the NYSE?

Because of the fact that the NASDAQ has been an electronic system, and the NYSE has been specialist-based. By not being electronically based, you never have the same kind of access to the markets on the NYSE—for now, anyway. In addition, the market maker structure on the NASDAQ gives you access to more information to follow and use to make your trades.

What do you think is in store for electronic trading in the future?

We are really at the very beginning. Three years from now, 10 times the number of people will be involved. So the people that get involved now and really learn the basics stand to capitalize on electronic trading for a long time.

Do you feel electronic trading will eventually be a global phenomenon?

Absolutely. Most of the markets around the world will end up being electronic, and you will have similar access and opportunities all over the world—and probably at all hours.

What are the trading rules that you live by?

Always play the percentages. The more you concentrate, the more successful you are going to be. Always be prepared; never walk into a day at 9:25 and expect to be successful. Recognize and identify trends and shifts; adjust your strategy based on market changes. You have to realize that the marketplace is changing constantly and you have to keep up with it the best you can.

7

LEARNING THE BASICS

—Scott Dishner

Scott Dishner recommends starting small. He says beginners should start by trading smaller, less volatile stocks, in less than 100-share increments, until they're completely comfortable with the market. By being disciplined, he has been able to walk the fine line between being patient and aggressive and doing very well in the process.

What is your personal electronic trading philosophy?

I try to make sure that I leave the office each day with more money than I had at the outset. This can be difficult when you see the potential that exists in the marketplace for doing very well, and when people around you are placing much larger trades. Where I get into trouble is when I'm up $2,000 on the day, but I want to be up $10,000 and I'm tempted to take on positions that are a little bit more of a gamble. Some of the Internet stocks move so quickly that all of a sudden they're down 10 points and you're out $5,000; that's when you think to yourself, "Damn, I wish I were still up $2,000." And some days I'll leave with $5,000 and think that I really missed some good opportunities that day, but I know that in the end, there will always be another opportunity to take advantage of. I try not to get too focused on each individual day, because then it becomes one day of euphoria followed the next by doomsday.

What do you look for in a stock?

The number one thing I want to see is who's buying the stock. I look to see which of the blue chip players, like Goldman Sachs, Morgan Stanley, and DLJ, are buying the stock and how much of it they are buying. I pay particular attention to when they are buying less expensive stocks. Stocks trading anywhere between $5 and $13 that have enough volume being traded, make for great opportunities to make a great transaction with limited risk. The larger stocks can be prohibitive, there are only so many shares of a $150 to $200 stock that you can buy. But if I can get my hands on 5,000 shares of a $12 stock on its way up to $15, I can make more money with a lot less risk of the stock diving 20 points in a matter of minutes.

What are some of the specific indicators that you use to determine when it's a good time to buy a stock?

I find that one of the most important things that we look for is price. By knowing the history of a particular stock, we find ranges in which we are comfortable buying the stock. Let1s say Yahoo! goes down to 160. We can see that it has dropped to the 160 range before, but has always bounced back up, so we know it's a good idea to buy at this price. It takes a lot of patience, because a lot of times you'll see Internet stocks rising and dropping full points in a matter of minutes.

When you're in a stock that you see is going down, what is your instinctive reaction?

It depends on how well I know the stock. If I don't really know a stock, and I just bought it because it looked like it was about to go up and I was wrong, I get out right away. If it's a stock that I trade a lot and understand, I will ride the stock down and look to buy more at that price and average down, or I will sell a part of it and hold onto the rest in order to mitigate my risk. Sometimes I'll even hold onto a stock after the market closes because I'm so sure that it's going to be right back up again the next day. It really depends on how well I know the stock and the way it has reacted to specific price levels and market information in the past.

Why do you often hear that electronic trading is so risky?

It's funny the misconceptions that people have about electronic traders. They stem from the fact that there are risks as well as amazing gains inherent in electronic trading. A lot of people lose money electronic trading because, naturally, a lot of people buy at the top and sell at the bottom. Those people, however, have no training and unrealistic expectations. You really have to sit down in front of the screen and learn the stocks, and very few people can just come into electronic trading and make money right away anymore. Chances are you will lose money in your first two to four months of trading. It is very difficult to learn the effects of market makers on a particular stock, previous support and resistance levels, and who the major players are within a particular stock.

There are also many different ways to buy a stock. For example, to buy a stock you could preference a market maker, buy it off the ECN or place a bid on Island. There are tons of different ways to place an order, and to be really good and get the best prices, you need to learn which ones are best for which situations. To use a sports analogy, if you're a basketball player and you're going to the hoop, there are many different ways for you to get to the basket and score. It depends on where the defenders are, who is open on your team, and your natural instinct whether to pass, pull up, and shoot, or take it to the hole and dunk. Only experience can tell you what to do. You have to build a capital base that allows you to take on more risk and place larger orders. Learning to become a successful electronic trader is all done through experience, and it does not happen overnight. Too many people become day traders expecting to make fortunes right off the bat.

What advice would you give someone starting out?

You have to have patience and you have to put in a lot of work. You can't just come in and assume that you're going to do well by risking your entire capital base and trading large amounts of highly volatile stocks. It is critical to learn the fundamentals by trading the smaller stocks that are less volatile until you're completely comfortable. You should never trade more than 100 shares of stock at a time in the beginning—and don't think that just because you're trading 100 shares of stock and making $75 a day that it's not worth your time. If you're too impatient and start trading larger amounts and losing lots of money, you're also going to lose confidence. When you lose confidence, you start hoping, and that's when things can get bad. You start placing random orders in an attempt to make a lot of money in a hurry, and that's too dangerous. My best advice is that you remain patient. Once you start getting a feel for it and making money on a consistent basis, you can start placing larger trades.

How have Internet stocks changed the market?

It's revolutionary. Even though the valuations are so high, individuals such as myself, who are prime candidates to use e-commerce, have only just started buying products and services over the Internet. Most people haven't even begun using it. I feel that the Internet stocks are going to continue to go up and a lot of the small Internet companies are going to be taken over by larger ones. Internet stocks provide an opportunity to make a lot of money every day. Before Internet stocks, it was semiconductors and biotech stocks. But a big day then was when a stock moved four whole points in a day. Now, we've got situations where stocks jump 40 points in a day. You can now hold 200 shares of a stock, watch the stock go up 20 points within a day, and make $4,000 right there. I used to have to trade with huge quantities of stock in order to make that much money. I would have to buy 2000 shares, because it would only be going up two points and I wanted to maximize my investments.

What do you think will happen to electronic trading if the market crashes?

Electronic traders are probably in the best position of all investors, if the market crashes. When you're trading electronically, you have the ability to quickly enter and exit a position. The biggest days I have had are following a day that the market is down. I usually come in the next morning licking my chops trying to buy everything I can, knowing that the market is going to bounce back. Even if it does not, I can quickly exit my positions and cut my losses. However, the majority of the time the market does bounce back. Of course a market crash is going to hurt everyone, but electronic traders can get out of positions much more quickly than the normal investor, so they're going to be hurt the least.

What is the best electronic trading advice you ever received?

The best advice I have ever received is that you have to learn to take losses and still be aggressive. Initially, it's all trial and error. Start small, because you're not going to get hurt too badly if you're only trading 100 shares of stock. By being active in the market and placing lots of trades, you will get the experience you need to be more confident.

What about the worst advice you have ever received?

The worst advice I have ever received—and I have to say that I've been very fortunate to have been surrounded by very good traders, so I haven't received too much bad advice—is for a new trader to try and mimic a more experienced trader. You're never going to be able to replicate someone else's style exactly, and you need to begin developing your own. There are definitely things you should be able to take away from a more experienced trader, but you should use them only as part of your overall trading strategy.

How different are the trading styles of each electronic trader?

I've never seen two people trade the same way. Once people learn the basics they begin developing their own individual style. Every trader looks for different indicators and interprets market data differently. The key is to develop a style that you are comfortable with and that you can adjust over time. The market is in a continuous state of change, so you need to be able to update your style as the market and technology advance.

So what is it that makes a successful electronic trader?

Being a successful electronic trader takes the right combination of patience, hunger, emotional detachment, and precision. You have to walk the fine line between having the patience to wait for stocks to fall into your buying zone and the confidence to be aggressive. It might sound contradictory to have to be both patient and aggressive, but that is what really successful traders are. I know a lot of successful traders who never had any exposure to the stock market before becoming an electronic trader. More than anything else, electronic trading has to do with personality and the ability to learn. You can sit there and read every investment and technical analysis book ever published, and that still does not mean you will be a successful electronic trader. You have to spend the time to learn and understand what it is that drives particular stocks.

Why are there so many misconceptions about electronic traders?

The misconceptions fall into two extremes: first, that it's too easy, and second, that it's impossible. But if you look at it, it's not at all easy. In order to succeed, you really need to understand what it is that drives particular stocks. I enjoy trading because it's such a challenge. You've always got to be studying your stocks and have your eyes peeled for information that could effect the price. Unfortunately, the public is misguided because of the way the media portrays electronic trading. They seem to feel that it is the same as online investing and they do not understand the distinct differences between the two. The only way you can really understand the full scope of this industry is to sit down in front of your computer and learn.

Are electronic traders good for the market?

Definitely, because we increase liquidity in the marketplace. Electronic traders are primarily in competition with the market makers. If anything, electronic traders provide price improvement for a lot of investors. The trading that we do only takes money out of the market makers' pockets because they can't make as much money on the spreads anymore.

Why is it that electronic traders trade primarily on the NASDAQ instead of the NYSE?

The NASDAQ is the market to be in for electronic traders because traders can get prints on the NASDAQ but not on the NYSE. The last few years, it has really outperformed the NYSE in many ways. The NYSE seems to be more of an old-boy network that's more concerned with price-to-earning ratios and multiples of earnings that are important for long term technical analysis. Day trading is all about intra-day movement, and with the incredible volatility of Internet stocks, long term analysis goes out the window. Almost all of the Internet companies list on the NASDAQ. Take a look at where the future is. It's in technology, and the NASDAQ is a technology driven marketplace. It is slowly but surely becoming the number one market in the U.S.

8

THE ELECTRONIC TRADER'S ADVANTAGE

—*Kirk Kazazian*

KIRK KAZAZIAN WAS PREMED IN COLLEGE BUT WANTED A WALL STREET-TYPE EXPERIENCE BEFORE GOING TO MEDICAL SCHOOL. HE ENDED UP AT A DAY TRADING FIRM, AND STILL HASN'T LEFT. RECOGNIZING THE POWERFUL ADVANTAGE ELECTRONIC TRADERS HAVE OVER ONLINE INVESTORS HE HAS BEEN ABLE TO PROFIT FROM THE INCREDIBLE VOLATILITY THAT EXISTS IN TODAY'S MARKET.

How would you explain electronic trading to a normal investor?

Electronic trading is really about being able to take advantage of the volatility that exists in today's stock market. Most investors see their stocks go up or down gradually over time, but are unaware of the major fluctuations that occur over the course of a single day. Especially with the effect of online investing, there are more trades being placed every day, which makes for more volatility in the market as a whole. The advances in technology, coupled with regulations put on traditional brokerage firms, have created an entirely new market for trading stocks. You can now trade directly with other individuals. There is no need to place an order with a third party, like a broker or an online investor network. You can now have access to the same information that professional traders on Wall Street use, and trade with them directly instead of paying someone else to place the trade for you.

How is this different from investing online?

When using an online brokerage firm, you are still placing your trade through a third party. The price you are quoted for a stock is not necessarily the price you are going to be able to buy the stock at. Electronic traders are able to see the actual prices the stock is being offered for. This is called the offer price. We then hit the stock directly, and we own it. This all happens in the course of about three seconds. When investing online, you have to wait minutes or hours to find out if you are actually able to buy a stock. This is because you place an order online, the message is conveyed to an individual on the floor of the exchange, and then that individual buys the stock for you. Electronic trading software allows you to see the price a stock is being offered for and to buy it immediately. As of right now you have to trade in 100-block shares and there is no undo button, but it is the most direct and profitable way to invest. We will all some day be trading in this direct method, but most people do not understand what really happens when they buy a stock so they think electronic trading is a bad thing.

What does it take to make the jump from online investing to electronic trading?

Online investors trade more on fundamentals, while electronic traders trade on volatility. The key is to look at what other individuals and institutions are doing. As an electronic trader you have access to software that allows you to see the market in a stock. This means you can see who is going to bid high and who is going to bid low and make your own assumptions about how this will affect the price of the stock. Electronic traders really try to understand the personality of a stock, what makes it move, who the market makers are, and what price the stock has traded at over time. Becoming an electronic trader really entails being able to change your mentality to paying attention to what moves a stock. The electronic traders who make the most money are the ones who know a stock inside and out, meaning they can tell where the stock has traded over the last few years, how it reacts to certain pieces of news such as earnings and how it reacts to overall market trends. Day trading is something that is very difficult to do casually; you really need to get inside a stock to understand how to make money on it on a daily basis. It requires an incredible amount of discipline and time to really study the market and the particular stocks you follow.

How did you get into electronic trading?

I graduated a year early from school after being premed. I had always had an interest in the markets and wanted to have the "Wall Street" experience for a year or two before going into medicine. I heard about this new trading system that was beginning to transform the way trades were placed. Then, after hearing from a friend who was trading for a small firm about the massive amounts of money being made, I decided to investigate. It turns out that these traders all had one thing in common, and maybe only one thing in common: the desire to make a lot of money. They seemed to be pretty successful at it so I decided to give it a try.

Had you ever traded before?

I had invested my own money for quite some time, but trading is very different. I quickly learned how different it really was to be a trader instead of an investor. It was as if traders had the right information, the real time data and the inside knowledge of how to place stock trades. It was as if they were cheating compared to normal investors. I had never known that they had access to such information and what a difference it truly makes. Learning how to trade successfully is really more about having the right tools and absorbing the right information. So much can be learned just from watching successful traders and studying their habits. There is a science to it, but nobody can truly quantify it. Those that do get it can't always explain how, even if they are doing incredibly well.

What were your concerns about electronic trading?

From what the other electronic traders were telling me, it seemed too good to be true. I figured I would try it for a couple of weeks and find out if it was real and if there was really the chance to make all the money that everyone else was supposedly making. I was fortunate to be placed with a great trader when I first started. I cannot overemphasize how helpful this is when you are first starting out. Just by sitting next to him for three weeks, I was really able to learn a lot and begin defining my trading strategy. This enabled me to begin making money way before most electronic traders do when they first start. I tell everyone that you need to sit and learn for at least three to six months before you can expect to begin really making money. Those that expect to make too much too soon are the ones that really get burned.

What was it like when you first started electronic trading?

When I first started trading, SOES was the major network used by electronic traders. You could buy and sell stocks instantaneously, selling 1000-share blocks for point gains within 15 seconds. You could make money all day just by following a few simple rules. The marketplace changed in 1997 when ECNs came into existence and SOES became obsolete. SOES was more buying and selling based on imbalances that existed in a particular stock. The advent of ECNs as the preferred method of trading has really legitimized the art of electronic trading. We now evaluate the buyers and sellers in the market, research trends, examine momentum, and can trade in less than 1000-share blocks. Because you can now trade in 100-block shares, this has also opened the market a lot for other individuals to become electronic traders. In fact, I would recommend starting off in 200- to 300-block trades for the first couple of months until you are more experienced.

What were your first impressions of the job?

Electronic trading is a lot different from normal investing or online investing. Although I did not have that much money to start with, it is incredible how quickly it can grow or disappear. It was absolutely amazing how much money other people were making around me. The environment was incredibly fast-paced and I often found my head spinning. The amount of information flashing on the computer screen was still very confusing to me, but it began to make sense over time. Once you understand all of the symbols and blips on your screen, it is really not that confusing. You just have to be quick on the keyboard so you can enter and exit trades in a hurry. These traders were in a stock sometimes for only 10 seconds, making a quick eighth of a point and then looking for their next move.

How long did it take for you to feel as if you knew what you were doing?

It definitely took a couple of months before I knew what I was doing. There is really no way to tell when you understand what it takes to make money as a trader. Everything happens so quickly that one day you just sit back and realize that you have learned to piece together information to really understand what drives the market and the particular stocks you follow. The more time you spend doing it, the more aggressive you get. The key is to get over the initial fear factor and build a base of capital instead of worrying about how much money you make or lose with every trade.

What got you over the fear factor?

Your confidence grows over time. It really helped sitting next to more experienced electronic traders and studying the way they dissected market information. I didn't actually start trading for a month, which was very useful. I was able to develop a trading strategy and really set limits on how much I would stand to lose on a single trade or on a single day. After a couple of months I was consistently making money. At this point I had reassessed my risk levels and was trading with larger amounts of money, which allowed me to make that much more. It is really a game of building your confidence and capital base. If you can do this steadily over time you can do extremely well.

How do you handle the risk?

I never think about how much money I make or lose on one single trade. If you follow a set strategy, it is much easier to take emotions out of each individual trade. Therefore, I don't get too excited or too upset about any one trade. I just look for the certain criteria that I use every time when I buy or sell a stock. You may only be in a trade for 10 seconds, so you have to be able to know inherently how much you can afford to risk on any individual trade.

What are you thinking over the course of the day while you're trading?

Over the course of a day I am really focused on following all of the indicators that can affect my positions. This includes general market information, particular stock information, and the volume of trades being placed. The main thing I focus on is volatility, then liquidity. When volatility starts to decline, I'll get out of my positions. It is much more difficult to judge a stock when there is little volatility. Liquidity is what allows electronic traders to quickly enter and exit positions. Without it, we could get stuck in a position and lose a lot of money. The main advantage an electronic trader has is speed, so we look for stocks that are extremely liquid and have a lot of volatility.

Is there a set pattern to your trading style?

I am the most active in the first hour of the morning, when the market opens, and the last hour of the day, when the market closes. The market has been so volatile lately that it can absolutely reverse itself during these two periods of the day. Many traders look to initiate positions when the market opens or close out positions before the market closes so you see an incredible amount of activity during these times. I do not place as many trades between 11 and 1 because the liquidity tends to dry up. Also, one thing I've found with electronic trading is that very few people make money shorting a stock. It's especially tough to succeed if you are consistently betting on stocks going down: there's always a bottom to a stock, but there's never a limit to how high it can go.

What are the tools you need to be a good electronic trader?

A high-speed computer with an Internet connection speed is critical. Now, for the first time, you can use software from an electronic trading firm such as TRADESCAPE.*com* and have access to its interface from any computer. Each firm's computer system is geared toward something specific. Ours is geared more towards rapid trading and high volume, so we get in and out of positions very quickly. Other places may use a lot of graphs, and will have things like trade alerts and price alerts. It really helps to get involved with an electronic trading firm because you can often learn from some of their more experienced traders. Some places will even put up some capital to support you in return for part of your winnings. So the first thing to do is to find a place that has a good system, a fast connection to the Internet, and where people are actually making money.

How important is discipline in what you do?

Discipline is everything. It comes with confidence, because once you know you can make money every day, you're not afraid to take a loss. Not having discipline is a recipe for absolute disaster. That is why you hear about so many day traders who lose their shirts. If you have discipline and follow a set strategy, your risk level is so much lower. You can then slowly build up a capital base until you can afford to take bigger positions. No matter how convinced I am of a position, I always keep a reserve of buying power. There are many ways to discipline yourself and still allow yourself to go for large positions when you are absolutely convinced a stock is going to move a certain way.

How do you decide when to get out of a long position when it is going down?

Here's the problem: If you're in a stock that is slowly going down and the market is full of sellers trying to get out of the position, then I like to just sell. If I'm in a stock that's rapidly going down, not because there's news on it, but because there's a reaction to a big selling pressure in the market, usually there's going to be a big bounce back. A stock that's going down slowly tends to stay down, whereas a stock that plummets, as long as there's no bad news, will usually swing right back up again. It doesn't matter if the market makes wild swings, as long as there's liquidity and volume.

How has increased liquidity in the markets helped electronic traders?

The number of individuals trading and investing has drastically increased. One of the biggest factors has been the rise of millions of online investors, who are placing more trades than ever before. This, coupled with the craze over "hot" Internet stocks, has greatly increased the liquidity of the market and created more opportunities than ever to make money. Electronic traders are at a great advantage over traditional investors, though, because we have the tools and access to instantaneous market information. Investors are blindly sending in buy and sell orders using limited information. It is impossible for them to judge the strength of a stock based on anything other than charts or delayed market information.

Electronic traders have access to real-time information. This means we can actually see the buyers and sellers in the marketplace, where they are bidding for a stock, and the volume of shares they are trading. This allows us to be able to determine where the stock is going in the next five seconds, five minutes or even five hours. It is really amazing how much more you can understand about a stock when you have access to true market data. It is no wonder that the professional traders on Wall Street have been doing so well for so many years and tried to prevent others from gaining access to this information.

What is it that you like most about electronic trading?

It's exciting, it's fun, and once you get good at it, the stress goes away. There is really no other job in the world that gives you the opportunity to make this much money on your own terms. As long as I don't do anything irresponsible or make a bad trade, I'm okay. If I follow my game plan and still lose money, I don't really mind, because I did what I was supposed to do. I don't like it when I make a stupid mistake—that really gets to me.

What are some of the common misconceptions about electronic trading?

The public is still so confused about what electronic trading is really all about. Even the media still confuses electronic trading with online investing. It is just a very new concept that, like anything else that is new, is going to take time for the general public to understand. People seem to be confused by the lack of rules governing electronic trading and the fact that to become an electronic trader requires no formal training, licenses, or experience. You take on 100 percent of the risk, but you also take home 100 percent of the rewards.

What advice would you give someone just starting out in electronic trading?

I would advise them to start out small, realize that they're not going to make money for a while, and study the market. In each situation where you buy or sell a stock, you must evaluate the marketplace. It is also incredibly important to be extremely fast on the keyboard. You must be able to enter and exit trades in seconds, which requires knowing exactly which keys to press and all the shortcuts you can use. In addition, there are the things you can't really teach. You have to be open-eyed, quick and attentive to patterns developing within a stock. You also have to not get flustered under pressure and be able to take a loss without being affected mentally.

What do the good traders do that distinguishes them from the rest?

Good electronic traders make decisions very quickly. They know what they're looking for and they jump on it when they see it. They are very perceptive and unemotional. I think that once a trader gets on a roll, he starts realizing what it is that makes him so good and starts acting accordingly.

What do you see as the future of electronic trading?

Electronic trading has changed a lot over the last couple of years. The rules used to be a lot more rigid than they are today. For the first time ever, any individual can gain access to the same tools as the professional traders on Wall Street. There will continue to be the development of additional ECNs, allowing more and more individuals to have direct access to the marketplace. Whether they officially call themselves electronic traders or not is another story, but the markets in general are moving towards a more direct model.

9

THE MILLION-DOLLAR OPPORTUNITY

—*Jason Rosen*

J ASON ROSEN SEES ELECTRONIC TRADING AS A BATTLE OF THE MINDS, WITH EVERYONE LOOKING FOR THE SAME CLUES. HE HAS PROSPERED BY BEING LIGHTNING QUICK ON THE KEYBOARD AND ABLE TO ALTER HIS STRATEGY ON A SECOND'S NOTICE. FOR JASON, THE EXCITEMENT AND COMPETITION OF ELECTRONIC TRADING MAKE IT THE GREATEST OPPORTUNITY IN THE WORLD, AND THE BEST WAY TO WIN IS TO DETACH ONESELF FROM THE MONETARY VALUE AND FOLLOW A STRICT DISCIPLINE.

How did you get into electronic trading?

I got started through a friend who kept regaling me with stories of how well he was doing at this small electronic trading firm on Wall Street. So after listening to him for months and growing tired of my consulting job at JP Morgan, I decided to take a chance. It sounded like what he was doing was legitimate, and I was at a place in my career where I could take a chance. I kind of looked at myself and thought, "Am I going to work at this place for five years, become a principal, and someday a vice president?" I could have stayed there and built up my resume, but I had gotten into that job because it was what there was to do, not what I wanted to do.

Can you explain day trading?

Well, what we try to accomplish is to capitalize on the daily fluctuations of stocks. Stocks will fluctuate all day long, and someone can open up the paper the next day and see a stock that finished up a half a point on the day. They have no idea that the stock might have been up four points, down three, up one, down two, then up a half. For example, if you're looking at a stock with a price of $60 a share that may trade within an eight-point range ($56 to $64), in that range it could make the equivalent of 30 points worth of moves in a day. So theoretically, while the stock only went up one or two percent of its value that day, 50 percent of the stock was actually traded in terms of points. Basically, a day trader will try to take advantage of all those changes on an individual basis.

It's a cycle of patterns, so electronic trading might be the most raw way to take advantage of the ability to see and predict those patterns and capitalize on the daily fluctuation in the market. Everybody's trying to do that; everybody wants to buy low and sell high. For example, normal investors will buy Intel at 110 and sell it when it hits 125 for a 15 point gain. However, within the time that the stock went up 15 points, there were times when it was down as well as up. We're watching it 100 percent of the time, in order to capitalize on 100 percent of the fluctuations.

What was it like when you first started electronic trading?

Some people would come in and figure it out really quickly, even within a month. It took me about three months to understand what it was all about, and then it took me about another three months to start making money. I think it was in my sixth month that I posted my first real profitable day. I started out trading 1,000 block shares of stock that were valued under $50, because those stocks are a lot less volatile. Early on, we would try getting in and out of stocks quickly for only a quarter or a half point, and if you made enough good trades over a day you had the potential to make $500 to $1,000 a day.

How many trades were you doing a day?

Early on I probably made about 50 or 60 trades in a day. But that was early on. I make well over 200 trades a day now, which ends up being about 200,000 shares a day. On my biggest day ever I traded about 496,000 shares.

Do you follow a certain set group of stocks?

Only Internet stocks on the NASDAQ. There's so much volatility in Internet stocks on a daily basis that it guarantees the opportunity to make money.

How do you handle the ups and downs during the course of a day?

The only way that you can be successful is to completely remove yourself from the money. You have to remove yourself from the actual monetary value of the numbers that are on your screen. I approach it as a video game until the end of the day when I see the final numbers.

Do you follow a set strategy?

There's not really a set strategy I use. I approach it more on a daily basis, and I'm one of the electronic traders with the least ability to think long-term. Because I have so little patience, I need to take everything as it comes. I'm constantly re-evaluating my situation and strategy over the course of a week or even a day. One of the key traits of being a successful trader is being able to adjust to new market conditions. You always have to adjust if you want to remain a successful trader over the years.

How long are you in a stock?

Sometimes I am in a stock for five, six, or even 10 minutes, but it is entirely different for each electronic trader. Sometimes I build positions over a while and try to get a hold of the stock in anticipation that it will really go up. Then there are times when I'll be in a position for 10 to 15 seconds and then quickly try and get back in again.

Does each trader have his own different strategy?

Yes, it's pretty varied from one trader to the next. My strategy is a lot different than other traders' because I think I'm one of the fastest in terms of making split-second decisions and executing to get into and out of stocks. My eyes are always locked in on my screen with my fingers constantly moving on the keyboard. In fact, I have a little bit of a nervous twitch where I just sit there and nail the tab key all day long because it highlights the little boxes. I'm almost like a windup toy.

I think my ability to look into the immediate future has really fueled my success as an electronic trader. It's like chess, where some people may be able to only look ahead three or four moves. But I can see over 10 moves ahead and know how to react differently. I have one of the better abilities to anticipate what's going to happen in the immediate future, and basically I calculate what I'm going to do in each situation as it approaches. So as I am playing out one of my positions in the market, I am immediately executing my moves according to what I've preplanned.

When I'm trading I'm really focused; my hands are lightning on the keyboard. You have to know exactly what button you're going to press in order to execute a specific transaction. If you want to buy, there are four major methods of buying (Island, InstaNet, SelectNet, SOES), so you've got to know which method you're going to choose for each different situation. You not only have to hit the keys quickly, but even more importantly, accurately. My strategy is to anticipate the future movements of a particular stock and then attack. I'm a very psychological trader. I try to figure out what the psychology of the masses is. You can see it on the screen: you can see panic or reluctance to sell, ultimately telling you what people are going to do before they even know to do it.

How would you describe the electronic trading culture?

It is kind of funny, where I work at TRADESCAPE.*com* everybody likes to play computer games. We're very competitive, but as if we were all playing a video game against each other. However, we're all in the game together for the same purpose and we are not actually competing against each other. On the personal level, it tends to be very laid back and everyone seems to get along really well. We're all in the same boat.

Is there such a thing as monotony in electronic trading?

Every day in this job you wake up knowing that something new is going to happen. You absolutely never know what can happen on any given day. With each new amazing event that surprises you, something even twice as incredible could happen the next day. This is what makes being an electronic trader so exciting.

What makes for a good trading day?

On any given day, all I need is just one stock to fluctuate a lot and I can make money. For example, a month ago the online brokerage stocks were going through the roof, even though the market in general was extremely idle. All I had to do was watch one stock, and the stock went from 25 up to 75 and then down to 35. That's enough for me to focus my entire day on. Usually there are one or two things every day which I really focus on. These stocks generally run independently of the market.

How would you characterize the type of people who are electronic traders?

They are the types of people who don't enjoy working for a boss, who want to be self-fulfilling; they're very competitive people who want to succeed and who don't want to follow a typical career path. It's a career where the sky's the limit; a commission-based career with few guidelines and tangible results.

How hard is it to get started as an electronic trader?

As far as a career goes, you have to be willing to pay your dues. I think anybody can do this. Basically, I was a very bad trader when I started. It literally took me three months to figure out what a stock was and why its price changed. I didn't understand the financials of companies and how the middlemen affected the price. However, by treating it as a career I really concentrated on remaining positive and committing myself to learning the fundamentals. And boy, has it paid off. If you follow the basic rules of this job, there is no reason why you can't make a fantastic living and make money every day.

What would you say is the key to success when starting out as an electronic trader?

The absolute fundamental key is to learn you can't trade on emotion. You have to trade on tendencies, odds, and predetermined rules you set for yourself. There are a lot of things that you don't realize you're going to have to learn, and it takes a lot of time to learn them. For example, you have to learn how to take a loss. When somebody takes a big loss, it's actually a very good learning experience. Once you get beyond that loss, you learn how to overcome the downs and turn them into gains the next time. Try to focus on a core group of stocks so that you begin to learn their behavior. By being patient and watching your stocks every day you will eventually learn the tricks of the trade.

What does your accuracy have to be to make money?

There are different strategies about accuracy. I personally have 50 percent accuracy on about 90 percent of my trades. This is my break-even money. My strategy is to use that money to "test the waters." Then I expect 10 percent accuracy on my other 10 percent of my trades. These are the big money trades that I really dig in. I often lose $125 on 8 trades in a row and make $5000 on the ninth. Electronic traders should always limit their losses and let their gains run.

How is it when you are having a losing day?

When I have a losing day, I think how could I lose all that money? But when I have a normal day, I really don't think anything of it. There are traders at our company who show up every day, who are extremely disciplined, and make money every day. They're not putting everything they own on the line. They've just developed their skills over time and they really understand what to do.

What do you think was one of your best days as an electronic trader?

I had been watching a stock, EntreMed, for a matter of months when the company released news that it had possibly found a cure for cancer. This was definitely one of my break-out days that really gave me the confidence to know I could make it in this business. I just happened to be right, not lucky, that day, and everything clicked into place. The stock had closed the day before at 13, and when we showed up to work the next morning it opened at 45. Then it was up to 50, then 60, then 70—all before 9:30 AM. By 9:30 the stock was up to $81, up almost 70 points. It came down to about 75 or so and then just hovered there for a while. I finally decide to short 1,000 shares of the stock in anticipation that it was going to dive. I shorted the stock at 75, from where it fell to 60 within seconds. I then shorted the stock again at 65 and it plummet-ed to 45. I had already made money and was able to take on risk. As soon as it didn't bounce back as people wanted it to, I just sat back in my chair and watched. I didn't even touch my keyboard. I just sat there. Look at it go. The dollar amount that was up on the screen kept going up from $10,000 to $11,000 to $12,000, and so on. The next thing I knew, I was up $40,000—only by trading these 1,000 shares. Seeing the vol-ume start to pick up again, I bought 1,000 shares at 45 and then sold when it ran up to 55. Once again, I saw the waver-ing in the market and I shorted it again at 55, from where it eventually fell to 50. I kept this up over the course of three hours, being right almost 80 percent of the time just by under-standing the psychology of the stock and the individuals who were buying and selling. I made over $75,000 that day alone.

On another day a couple of months ago, when the Brazilian currency was devalued, the market really took a dive. Yahoo! was down from 410 to 325 and Lycos was down from 110 to 75, just to name a few. Things were down big, but when I walked into work the following morning I was licking my chops, thinking, "I am going to buy like crazy today." Within five minutes I probably already had about one and a half mil-lion dollars in the market. I bought 1,000 shares of Amazon and Yahoo!, 2,000 shares of Lycos, and 3,000 of Excite. Anything I could get my hands on, I was buying. What ended up happening was actually a bit worrisome. The stocks all started to rise and all of a sudden started to plummet. Just as I thought I was going to lose a fortune, the stocks rebounded and went through the roof. This all happened over the course of an hour. Yahoo! for example had moved 80 points that morning. Stocks can take years to go up 80 points. If you're a trader, you literally show up every day hoping there is going to be a day like this—a day that will make your year.

When do you know that you have what it takes to trade successfully?

It is almost like driving a manual car for the first time. For a while, you don't get it and you bounce around a bit and stall the car. Then, all of a sudden, you finally get it and can't understand how you were ever unable to do it. I think that you just start to understand what drives particular stock movements and then can predict the movement of the stock price. It comes to a point where there's just nothing you haven't seen before. It's kind of like a chess game or a battle of minds, because if everyone's starting to look for the same clues, obviously they become harder to find. Everybody's driving for the same thing; however, nobody knows if it's going to go up or down.

What does it take to get started?

I think it takes a couple of months of believing that you're not going to make any money and dedicating yourself to understanding particular stocks. You're going to see other people making money and you've got to concentrate on yourself only, and not wonder about things you could have done differently. You just have to sit down and learn the fundamentals. Don't expect to become a master in your first month or two.

Do you enjoy electronic trading as a career?

I've done very well, and I love it. I could literally do this for the rest of my life: just wake up in the morning, trade for an hour and a half in the morning, make three or four thousand dollars, and go enjoy the rest of my day. It's the greatest job in the world when things are working out.

How do you continue to improve as an electronic trader?

The more I trade the more I commit to memory. Every day I learn something new and there is less that I have not seen in the markets. My goal is to experience each situation in the markets and digest the right pieces of information to allow me to capitalize on opportunities in the market as a whole.

What do you see as the future of electronic trading?

Initially, a bunch of people had the markets all locked up and were making a killing since the inception of the NYSE and the NASDAQ. Now it seems as though the walls are coming down more to let the normal investor in to take advantage of some of the riches. Eventually the walls will tumble completely and it will be happening on a global basis. Everyone wants to have control of his or her money and buy stock at the best price possible. Everybody will be electronic trading in one form or another some day very soon.

10

ELECTRONIC TRADING TOOLS

—Jeffrey Hooper

ELECTRONIC TRADING TOOLS ARE MUCH BETTER NOW THAN THEY WERE WHEN JEFFREY HOOPER STARTED TRADING SEVERAL YEARS AGO. HE BELIEVES THE MOST IMPORTANT THING TO LOOK FOR IN AN ELECTRONIC TRADING FIRM IS SUPERIOR TECHNOLOGY. OTHER KEY RESOURCES ARE YOUR FELLOW TRADERS AND YOUR OWN PAST EXPERIENCE. JEFFREY HAS BECOME SUCCESSFUL BY CONSTANTLY REVIEWING AND LEARNING FROM HIS TRADES OF THE PREVIOUS DAY BEFORE THE MARKETS OPEN EACH MORNING.

What was it like when you first started electronic trading?

When I first started, it was a totally different ballgame because we didn't have ECNs and we didn't have Island, which are now the primary tools for all electronic traders. There was something called SelectNet, which we still have, which was the negotiating system on the NASDAQ. There was SOES, which was automatic: We would buy on SOES, force our way in, and then negotiate our stock on SelectNet. Now SOES is secondary to everything else. There are now also better regulatory measures so the market makers will honor their markets more than they used to. NASDAQ used to be the red-headed stepchild of the trading world, but now it's earned a place of more esteem. Back then, we would really watch market maker movement; we would watch what Morgan Stanley and Goldman Sachs did. If they went to bid or went high bid on stocks that we like to trade, we would go there too, and we would look to pick up a thousand shares for a quick profit.

How do you monitor the stocks that you actively trade?

Then and now, we use what's called a ticker. It shows where a stock is going and the inside movements of a stock. It's very important—you always watch your ticker for market makers who are going to the bid and going to a new high bid. And all the while, you're looking for the spread, the difference between the bid and the ask, to be very narrow. Normally when stocks are at rest, they're not moving and have a certain spread—let's say 1/2 a point. On a 1/2 point spread stock, that spread tightens to 1/8 or 1/4 when volatility enters the picture. Volatility exerts pressure one way or the other. And when there's a high bid or market makers are leading the offer, it forces the pressure upward, and the stock price rises. The beautiful thing about SOES and now SelectNet Preference, is that an electronic trader who is quick and astute can force his way into the market.

What are the sources of information that are most important for you to have at your disposal?

It is incredibly helpful to be around other electronic traders. Personally, I could take or leave CNBC, but I like to hear what some of the insiders are saying about the markets. I read the New York Times and maybe Barron's on the weekends, but what makes me money is focusing on what market makers are doing on my screen.

How many positions are you in at any given moment?

I used to try to be in more than one stock at a time—10 stocks with 500 or 1,000 shares in each—but now I only trade one stock at a time because the market is so different and volatile. You need to be able to change your mind every 5, 10, 15 seconds—not just on a micro level, like buy or sell—but as a matter of changing your total focus. Flexibility is so key in this business.

How would you describe your electronic trading strategy?

I'm really looking for highly volatile stocks. I follow their momentum very closely and buy them on the way up and short them, if possible, on the way down.

How often do you go long in stocks as compared to going short?

About 75-80 percent of my trading is long. In most of the new issues you can't go short, and that is where I make a lot of my money.

How do you protect yourself against losses?

Whenever I buy a stock, I'm looking for very specific things to happen. The only way I'm going to buy a stock is if there is a strong bid and I think it is going to go up. If that stock doesn't go up, I sell it immediately. It either goes up, and I sell it in 20 seconds, or it doesn't go up and I sell it in 20 seconds. It is most important to have a set of values and stick to them religiously. It means defining your parameters for risk. Losses come from people not just being stupid, but being stubborn— for holding on to something because they've convinced themselves of something that's not necessarily true. The price doesn't lie. I've trained traders, and I've been absolute about it: You can't buy 1000 shares of a stock and watch it go down two points. I don't care what the stock is. In day trading, that's morally wrong.

When you start training someone new, what are the first major points you cover?

I want them to have an understanding of what they are doing, that the object of the profession is to make money, and that you need to do whatever you have to do within the confines of the rules and the limits of your capital to make money. Find a system that works. My system is to buy them on the way up and sell them on the way down. I want them to get an understanding of how the stocks move, how to pick out who the market makers are and what they're doing.

How much of an understanding of the financial markets is necessary to get into electronic trading?

I don't think that it helps to have any background in finances at all. I think it probably hurts because you have too many preconceived notions of what's going on. Day trading, in its purest form, is so far removed from all of that. The way we play it, it is a momentum game. If you're used to paying attention to what analysts say about stocks, you could put too much value on their guesswork. The only thing you can really get from an analyst is a hint that a stock might be ready to move. I learned my lesson early from paying too much attention to what an analyst said in Barrons: He mentioned something about a stock being upgraded, and I was watching it the next day. When it made the slightest movement, I bought a bunch of it and it went straight down. The research report was about three weeks old; in this business, news becomes old only moments after it breaks.

So you really need to trade with real-time information?

Definitely. And the best information that you can get is from other traders who are in the profession. Also, a rule of thumb in this business is that we will always want guys who are really competitive—whether it is sports or chess—and we'll take them over the top-flight scientists or engineers any day. There really is a competitive nature to day trading.

What are some of the skills that make for a successful electronic trader?

An asset that might seem superficial to this field but is really integral, is being able to type very quickly. Quickness is the name of the game. Both my parents are journalists, so when I was young, my parents encouraged me to learn how to type. I was typing 30 words per minute by the time I was 13. When I took typing classes in high school, I got myself up to 60 WPM. When I started electronic trading in 1994, I was so grateful for my ability to fly across the keyboard, because it really enabled me to stay on the very top of my trades. It's funny that part of my success as a electronic trader is due to my father's insistence that I learn how to type so that at the very least, when I graduated high school, I would have a marketable skill.

What is your advice on what someone's routine should be for the first several months?

I would make sure any novice has low expectations. But the most important thing might be to surround yourself with knowledgeable traders who know what they're doing. It's kind of like speaking a foreign language: When you're first learning a foreign language, you might know how to say hello and goodbye and conjugate a couple of verbs, but you really can't hold your own in a conversation; you can't put it all together. When you're first electronic trading, you might know the elements of trading—how to sell and how to buy—but you don't know how to do it so that you're making money. The key is to stick with it and be diligent about watching that screen, from before the open to the close of the day. Start small, and be confident that you will eventually get the hang of it.

What are some good types of stocks to start off with?

The main thing to keep an eye on is the spread. The spread is directly proportional to risk, the way that price is linked to volatility. You want to start with lower-dollar stocks—maybe $30 and under—and spreads that are a quarter point or less. That way if you're wrong, which beginners often are, and you're trading with 100 shares, you're only losing $25. You should start small, because essentially all stocks behave the same way: the bid straightens up, the spread narrows, the offer lifts. So if you're learning on a smaller stock, you have a better chance of figuring it out. I started out on a stock that was trading at about $30 to $40. I watched it all day long and was long and short in it at different times of the day. I really focused on that one stock to get a feel for how it moved. And I was able to understand the movements of the market makers within the stock. Eventually, I was able to use that knowledge and apply it to other stocks down the road.

How did you interpret the market maker's movements?

I saw which market makers would influence the stock's movement, and how they acted within that stock. I realized that those market makers probably represented institutional buy and sell orders, and that those orders were large enough that they probably took days to fill, thus driving gradual upward pressure on the stock.

How do you get ready for the market opening?

I read the New York Times for about 10 minutes and then I try to review my trades from the day before. I look over what I've done the day before and I punch them all up to see where they are at 8:30 the next morning—an hour before the market opens—and make a mental note of where they closed, where they're opening, who's on the bid. I take a mental snapshot of the 10 or 20 stocks that I'm in on a regular basis. About 9 AM, the ECNs are open for business and you can trade with them even though the market does not open until 9:30 AM.

Is there a lot of movement before the market opens?

Sometimes there is tremendous movement. If there's a merger announced, CNBC will be reporting the stock jump by 8:45 AM. And sometimes it doesn't even have to trade a share for the price to be moving. Sometimes the demand is such that it drives the stock price up before the market even opens.

What should someone look for in an electronic trading firm?

He should look for a firm with a good reputation and a lot of traders. Successful traders go to the best electronic trading firms and that is where you want to be. You also want to learn about the systems they use and have it written in stone what you're paying for commissions. You don't need a graphic function; you need a function that watches stocks based on color. Green is good; red is bad.

How does an ECN differ from SOES or SelectNet?

It's the other side of the market. An ECN is an order book, in that it shows all the bids and offers in a stock in that ECN. They are able to show you all their bids and offers. SelectNet, on the other hand, is how you buy from an ECN. You enter an order on SelectNet to buy from an ECN. It's like the ECNs are the garage, and SelectNet is the car.

There are so many ECNs and other transaction vehicles out there. How do you know which one to use?

If you're buying stock, you buy from the lowest offer. You don't care if it's Island, InstaNet, or any other ECN. And if you're selling, you look for the highest bid. The function of an ECN is similar to that of a market maker: They're representing orders in stocks. A trader's tools are SOES and SelectNet, and with those you can buy from and sell to any market maker or ECN.

How do you think a market crash would affect the liquidity and volatility of the stocks that you trade?

We've had some corrections since I've been trading, where people get jumpy and the online investors tend to exit the market. It's not so good for us, but I was making a living when the NASDAQ was trading only 150 million shares a day. There is still so much opportunity in the market, even if it goes from a billion to 750 million shares a day.

Do you need any type of license to become an electronic trader?

I think they're working on something called a Series 55, which will become the new electronic trading license. However, for now, you do not need any licenses.

What are the physical tools that you need to day trade?

Aside from a substantial sum of money, you need a Level-II work station as well as a system that watches the stocks. You also need a high-speed connection for the really quick in-and-out trading.

What exactly do Level-II quotes show you?

Level-II shows the inside market—all the market makers' quotes and other activity within a stock. An E*TRADE screen might show you what's called a Level-1 screen—the bid and the ask—but that's about it. A Level-II shows you where everyone is.

Do you feel that it is helpful to trade around other traders, or would you rather trade from home?

I'd much rather be on a trading floor. There's a reason that they're big, open rooms: Information is vital, and the best information is from people who are doing the same thing you're doing. I'm not saying that you can't make money using software at home. I'm just saying that if you want to be at the top of the day trading game, you need to surround yourself with other traders who are doing the same thing.

Are there ways to day trade without devoting yourself full time? Can you just watch it in the morning for a couple of hours and make money?

You can make money doing that, but you're just not going to maximize your potential. The online software is going to be useful for the part-time online trader who isn't really watching the market on a moment-to-moment basis. It's a great tool for online investors because the prices are very similar and the speed is twice as fast as what online traders normally work with. The at-home software is really a hybrid tool: it's got components of electronic trading, but it's based on an Internet function.

What skills are transferable from online investing to electronic trading?

It's hard to say, because all the basic rules of trading have been broken recently; there is little correlation between earnings and price, and stocks can go up and down without reason. That's an electronic trader's paradise: We make all our money when things are out of order. When an electronic trader sees a stock that's not where it should be, he doesn't say, "Oh, look, the stock is up 20, it's probably going to go down." We say "It could go up to 30 or 40—who knows?"

How would you describe the mentality of a successful electronic trader?

There's a certain amount of brain-picking before you can come up with your own trading strategy; you have to have a mold before you can break it. I didn't stick with the strategy of the guy that trained me, but I did keep about 75 percent of it. His strategy was more of a market strategy: When the market started to go up, he'd buy anything he could get his hands on. I'd rather concentrate more on the volatility of individual stocks. When the market went down, he could get caught, whereas I remained flexible. I'd be short, I'd be long, I'd go short again.

How would you describe the difference between electronic trading strategies?

There are traders like myself who just trade the stocks that are in play. Then I see some traders who trade the market as a whole, and then there are still others who are involved in a slower game of lower capitalization stocks that have a wider spread and are less risky. Those stocks might move quite a lot, but their movements are slower and based more on market maker movements, like the old-school style.

How much money do you feel you need to get started in day trading?

Nowadays I hear that you need at least $75,000 to start. You've got to have something to live off of, and you've got to have something to invest, and you've got to be able to take some losses.

How has your strategy changed over time?

Since the market has got so many traders in it now, it's become less easy. I've moved to the one-stock strategy and away from playing the market. At one point, I tried to trade a lot of less volatile stocks at the same time because I could really watch them, but I found that even that wasn't as successful as really focusing on one really hot stock.

How do you rebound from making a bad trade or hitting a losing streak?

I rebound by trying to make really simple, clean trades back-to-back. Trading is a lot like athletics: You just start to get in a zone, and you're overwhelmed with this emotion and this confidence. Good trading breeds more good trading; carelessness and stubbornness beget more carelessness and stubbornness. When you get in a bad streak, you just need to take a step back and wipe the slate clean. You need to get back to your fundamentals so that you can put three or four good trades together. Then you need to extend those trades out for three or four days, until you've built your foundation up again. Then you can start getting aggressive and taking more risks.

The key to nipping those bad streaks in the bud is to recognize them intra-day, and not to waste any time by digging yourself in deeper. When I first started trading, there was a whole year when I never ended up the day with a negative number on my screen, because my approach to each day was so ritualized. I came into each day in the same frame of mind, starting on a positive outcome from the previous day. I was able to see when I was starting to trade poorly, so that I could step away from my desk and come back fresh and trade the right way. It seems like all numbers and games when you're sitting in front of your computer, so it's easy to lose site of the fact that it's real money that you're trading with.

Can trading skills be taught, or are they absorbed and developed by each individual trader?

I think 75 percent of the early stuff can be taught, maybe even 90 percent, but down the line, each individual trader will develop his own system. There are really good teachers out there, but the best teachers are the ones who say, "I'll teach you, but once you start getting good, I want a cut of what you make," not the ones who say "Pay me $5,000 and I'll teach you."

Why do people fail as electronic traders?

I think arrogance is the main reason why people lose money, period. If you have the mentality that you know it all, you're definitely going to be wrong. Even now, the only thing that I know for sure in trading is that I don't really know anything. My success comes in being able to recognize a good trade and jumping on it as soon as I see it. Once I close it out, however, I go back to knowing nothing again.

How long do you typically hold your positions for?

Sometimes up to a minute.

Are you using all your capital to trade every day, or have you established a more balanced portfolio?

I trade with $400,000, which gives me about $800,000 in buying power, and that's plenty for me. When I have a couple of good months, I get to put away a little extra.

What role is electronic trading going to play in impacting the financial markets?

I've always felt like we were on the fringe. We used to call our-
selves "SOES Bandits," like we were on the outside, not really having any effect on the market. But now I see our role
expanding, because I think, innately, everyone wants to be
involved. Maybe not at the level that we are, but at some
level. Why wouldn't you want to have that kind of access to
the market? It's nothing less than a revolution.

**There are only a handful of ECNs in existence
now. Do you think that there will be a bunch
more popping up in the near future?**

Right now it's sort of a gold-rush mentality. Just like in the
1920s, there were only about 30 car manufacturers, and
now.... The life blood of ECNs is order flow, so only a few of the
existing ones will survive, like InstaNet and Island. The rest
will come and go, because it's an order book, and if you don't
have orders, you don't have a book. There is no time like the
present for electronic traders.

11

THE MASTER

—David Lu

David Lu first started trading using the telephone out of his home in high school. His knowledge of the markets has continued to grow since then; one of his strongest assets is his willingness to let trading consume his life. He says that much of his expertise comes from trial and error. He can make fine-tuned adjustments because of his experience with individual stocks, even if that means taking a loss to learn about them. He has since become one of the most successful electronic traders ever.

How did you first become interested in electronic trading?

It started when I was in high school. I was following investments and the Internet in general. My parents opened a joint account into which I could put some money. I started with some mutual funds, and then put some money into individual stocks. I did a little over-the-phone, touch-tone trading out of my house. It wasn't nearly the online or electronic trading of today; the technology wasn't there. But I was able to catch a few good stocks and be successful with them. After I had been trading stocks for a while, I started trading options and realized that I could make a lot of money doing that, even with a limited capital base.

What was trading like back then?

Some of the stocks I only held for short periods of time—like a day or so—but even though I knew SOES was going on, I wasn't able to capitalize on the speed of that technology. Not having access to this prevented me from taking more precarious short-term positions. I felt that I could probably do it, but over the phone it was really too slow, so that's what really got me interested in electronic trading.

It seems like you had a pretty solid investing background before you got into electronic trading. Do you think that's something everyone needs to have?

I've seen electronic traders who didn't have much of a background in investing get into the field, pick it up as they go, and end up making a good living. I wouldn't say it's imperative that you know the markets inside and out before you get into electronic trading, but you need to be able to pick it up somehow. Everybody really has his own unique method and style of electronic trading.

**And how would you describe your personal style
of electronic trading now?**

I think I do a little bit of everything, perhaps focusing a little
more on speed. I'm pretty quick on the keyboard. I probably go
a little bit further into the background of a company than most
people do. I tend to take a very diversified approach; I'm very
flexible in response to changing market situations. As more
and more players come in, the market becomes more evolved
and the regulatory structure undergoes some changes. My philosophy is really to be able to adapt to the changes in the market. I like to diversify my positions so that I have some that I
intend to hold for a minute or less, some hours, some days—
and a few I'll hold for weeks or months. Basically, I'm trying to
get as much out of each of my stocks as I can.

**What is the difference between a professional
electronic trader and someone actively investing
through the Internet?**

The difference between an electronic trader and someone
trading at home on Ameritrade or E*TRADE is that an electronic trader is trading from more of a short term perspective,
whereas an at-home online investor is in it more for the long
term.

**Can electronic trading exist outside of the very
volatile Internet stocks? Can people trade cotton,
for example?**

Well, in order for electronic trading to be effective and for people to make money doing it, there has to be a lot of volume—

which, of course, tends to cause volatility. On the exchange floor, there are people who are in the lumber pit—they are trading lumber, but there are really only a couple of individuals doing it because there's so little volume. They generally do the same thing as we do; they go out flat at the end of the day. But electronic trading will always tend to gravitate to areas with greater volume and volatility. As the barriers break down and the market makers continue to lose their monopolies on the floors, however, we will begin to see other markets for electronic trading and more individuals getting involved in the markets. As it is now, electronic trading exists on the NYSE, although the edge for electronic trading isn't as good as on the NASDAQ.

Do you think electronic trading is good for the markets?

I think it actually is good for the markets because before, when a customer wanted to place an order, the market makers could take advantage of the customers by using the window of information that only they had into the market place. Now, electronic traders are in the market to take the other sides of trades as well, so the customer gets a better fill, the electronic trader gets a better fill, and you've essentially eliminated the middle man. It works out better for everyone involved except, perhaps, for the market makers, who have had to relinquish their monopolies on the market place.

How has the role of the middleman or market maker evolved over the past couple of years?

On the NASDAQ, the changes over the last couple of years have really forced the spreads to narrow quite a bit, which has been to the detriment of the pockets of the market makers. Before, they would take a lot more positions, because the spreads were so wide that they could afford to take on more risk. Now there are many more market makers who just execute orders, and individual investors are taking more control of their positions in the market. It's basically allowed people more access to trade with each other at a much lower cost. Overall, for the market, it's definitely been a positive.

What is the effect of Internet stocks?

The Internet stocks are a little too young, partially because there are no earnings or the earnings are very low. Who's to say what the correct values of these stocks are, because they've all blown through the roof? And we have such a small amount of knowledge of what they're going to do in the future. Trading Internet stocks is like a game of hot potato. There certainly have been a great couple of days when new stocks were introduced and they skyrocketed for very short periods of time.

So what do you do after having those kinds of days? Do you discipline yourself to put it away, or do you just keep trading with it and sometimes throw all of your capital into the market?

On my best day, for example, I came into work, business as usual, and I had an incredible morning. One of the guys that I trade with mentioned that if he were me, he'd be out partying, celebrating, not wanting to lose it. However, on a day like that you have got to realize there's bound to be a lot of volatility in the market, and it is one of those rare opportunities to make even more money by having discipline, and not be tempted to lose it all.

How important is it to be continuously focused throughout the day?

Some of my coworkers can walk around and have lunch in the middle of the day. It's all too intense for me—I have to keep sitting there to watch everything as much as possible all day, because there's always that chance that something will happen without even a moment's notice. When something comes into play, at that point, that's the stuff that an electronic trader lives for. It's like hitting the sweet spot on a golf club or a tennis racket; it's when the reward is the greatest. And it can happen at any time. For example, if a biotech company comes out with FDA approval right in the middle of the day, you just have to be there to catch it. I mean, there are cases when a stock will double or triple within a matter of 30 minutes.

It sounds like you take a slightly different approach to electronic trading. While it seems that most electronic traders catch what comes and goes as it flits across their screens, you pay attention to the market as a whole and how it affects the stocks in which you might want to take positions. So, in doing this, what goes through your head?

I'm really just trying to figure out the puzzle. I take into consideration all the individual components. Like if Goldman Sachs starts selling a lot of stock, what's causing them to make that decision? What news is out there and how might it impact the Internet stocks? I try to fit together as many pieces of the puzzle as possible, and then I make my best judgment based on that information. In terms of managing risk, it's more difficult. You can't really think about the money all the time, because you don't want to get bogged down in that mentality. You also have to realize that you're going to take a lot of losses, no matter what. So you have to be careful to trade with no more than what you can afford to lose.

Do you take more losses than gains?

Maybe in terms of sheer number, but those losses are all small, so the gains outweigh them by far. I may lose a quarter of a point here and there, but then I'll gain a few points at a time.

Do you have a set strategy over the course of a day?

A lot of my decisions are really just based on my personal experience with how certain stocks react to the market and my feel for the market. It's mostly a gut feeling, and kind of hard to put into words. You develop a feeling for each stock and each position, and if you have a bad feeling, you get out.

What kinds of stocks are you trading?

Since the Internet started getting strong back in 1997, I've been trading a lot of Internet stocks—or rather, technology stocks in general.

How do you adjust your strategy so that you stay on top of a changing market and the advances being made in technology?

I think a lot of it is trial and error. You need to find out on your own what does and what doesn't work. Whenever I get into a position, I have a pretty good idea of what my downside risk is. I try to get into low-risk situations and get a good feel for a stock as soon as I take a position in it. I can basically trade any stock that's out there as long as it's volatile enough. I guess any adjustment I make comes from my experience with a particular stock, and my willingness to take a loss in order to learn more about it.

What advice would you give to new electronic traders just getting into the field?

I would advise that anyone who wants to get involved in electronic trading take it seriously. Treat it as a full-time job. It sounds great: You work from 9:30 to 4:00 and make a couple thousand dollars a day and then take off and go golfing, but you really need to let it consume your life. After the markets close, go over all the trades you've made that day, all the mistakes you've made, and reinforce the learning experience. A lot of people want to shove their mistakes aside—they'll lose a point on a stock, and then they'll want to be done with it and not think about it anymore. It's really important that you go over your mistakes and learn as much as you can from them, so that they serve their purpose. It's also important to learn as much as you can about the market in general. Read the paper; research the industry. A lot of people can get away without doing that part, but you do yourself a much greater service if you educate yourself.

How do you maintain your emotional edge?

I try not to get too emotional at all during the day. I will have the occasional outburst, where I curse and get upset, but I try to let go of it right away so that I can get back to being as calm as possible. If you get excited—either when something's going in your favor or going against you—it really affects your ability to reason and make the calm decision that you would have under normal circumstances. I try to eliminate the emotional aspect as much as possible. It's also really important to be able to bounce back from taking losses; some people can't do that, and it ruins their next hour's worth of trading. You can't let yourself carry over emotions from the last trade you've made into the present trade you're making. If you let yourself do that, you stray from your plan.

Why do you think it is that so many people question the legitimacy of day trading?

I think that a fair amount of the negative things that have been said about day trading have been said because of some level of jealousy. It's a very anti-establishment type of field. A lot of people who aren't well informed come into the industry and don't have the patience and the discipline to succeed, and they end up losing money and leaving the industry. If you're in your early 20s and you're coming out of college, you can work for a couple of years as an analyst, go to business school, or you can try your hand at day trading and see what happens. You can always start over if things don't work out. It was definitely hard to explain to my parents. For a while, they were sure I was doing something illegal, and that was when I was only telling them about a tenth of what I was making.

My dad would say, "Don't tell me—it'll only make me more nervous." I think, to a large extent, the problem lies with the people who scoff at the Internet having become such a big growth industry. And still, the large profits that people have made electronic trading don't really compare to the large profits that people have made from taking their companies public. It will be interesting to see how electronic trading does when the growth of the Internet slows down, which will eventually happen—although I hope not any time soon.

Could it be that because day traders are making considerably greater amounts of money than the market makers and brokerage firms have ever made before, the latter are getting jealous?

I would agree with that. Most of the establishment doesn't really have a presence in electronic trading, or even in online investing for that matter. They talk down electronic trading because it takes away from their core business, namely charging high-priced commissions to their customers. They're scared to get into it because it's going to erode their profits, even though the market as a whole is heading that way. They're scared of losing their client base, and the best way to prevent people from heading towards it is to portray it in a negative light. They say, "It's a sign of a bull market," or "It's totally based on speculation." It's easy to say all that and it makes them sound smart, but it's not well informed.

And for people who are scared off by that, it's probably better that they not get into day trading, because it's a pretty intense career and it takes a lot of effort. There are also these commercials for online brokerage firms which give the public the opposite impression—that it's too easy to make money, and that's not the way it is, either. Not only does it take a lot of work, but you also have to be emotionally and psychologically prepared for the ups and downs that are inherent in day trading. You don't really know until you try it, but you might be better off buying and holding than subjecting yourself to the pressures of making and losing thousands of dollars in a matter of seconds.

What is the best part of being an electronic trader?

I would say that the best part about it is that it allows individuals to participate in the market without having to work for a big firm. It really democratizes the whole trading process.

Do you see yourself doing this for a while?

Yes, I think so. I'll probably also move into some longer term investments, but there's still nothing like catching a stock in the middle of the day and making a big profit on it. That's something that I'm not ready to give up.

12

THE ELECTRONIC TRADING COMMITMENT

—Ed Lee

E D LEE HAS HAD A SUCCESSFUL CAREER AS AN ELECTRONIC TRADER OVER THE LAST TWO YEARS AND IS NOW MAKING THE MOVE TO MEDICAL SCHOOL. HIS DILIGENT HARD WORK BEFORE AND AFTER MARKET HOURS LED HIM TO COVER A WIDE RANGE OF STOCKS IN EVERY INDUSTRY. HE HAS SUCCESSFULLY TRANSITIONED FROM A FULL-TIME TO A PART-TIME ELECTRONIC TRADER AND EXPLAINS THE COMMITMENT LEVELS NECESSARY TO MAKE MONEY AT ANY LEVEL.

How did you get started in electronic trading?

I came out of Yale in 1996 and the only job I was offered was with a small electronic trading firm on Wall Street. I started out trading with their money and eventually moved on to trading with my own. However, when I started I really did not know anything about the financial markets at all. I actually did not even know the difference between a stock and a bond. I took a couple of classes at Rutgers University to learn some of the basics and really just absorbed information from other traders. So much of trading is just learning how to cut your losses and maximize your profits.

How hard was it for you to adapt without a finance background?

It really wasn't that hard because I really committed myself to making it work. A lot of people only come in part time and really do not spend the extra effort, but still make a decent living. Others really spend the time learning what it takes by reviewing trades and talking with other traders—those are the ones that stand the chance to make millions.

How different is the effort level between traders?

It really varies. Some people take this as a full time job while others only trade part time. It is extremely important to be realistic about what you can achieve if you are not putting in a full-time effort. You can still make a good living and some extra cash on a part time basis, but you should reduce your risk levels because you will not be monitoring your positions on a full time basis.

What is a typical day like?

When I first started I came in at about 8:00 and left at 6:00 to have time to get ready in the morning and review my trades in the evening. Now that I have decided to go back to medical school, I have really cut back and only come in at 9:00 and leave at 4:00. Because I am not spending as much time analyzing my trades and the market in general, I have cut back on my volume and risk levels in order to place more conservative trades.

What is it that you should do before the markets are open?

Before the markets are open you want to look at the specific stocks you are going to be watching throughout the day. Look for particular news stories that came out overnight or stocks that are releasing earnings. These two pieces of information are really all you need to have a good indication of the stocks that will have movement for the day. The purpose of spending time in the morning is to prepare yourself mentally so that when you see the specific opportunities you are looking for you can instinctively pull the trigger. It is so important to play out these situations in your head before the markets open so that you do not have to spend time analyzing when you see the opportunity—you just act. It is also important to set your downside losses for particular stocks and situations. A lot of people freeze when they are holding a position and they see it going down because they did not even consider what they would do in this circumstance.

What should you be doing after the markets close?

When the market closes you should be reviewing every one of your trades. So many traders just analyze their winning or losing trades, however it is really important to analyze all of them. As a trader, you need to be continuously updating your strategy and the only way to do this is to learn from your mistakes and understand what you did right on your winning trades. Talk to other traders about your positions and see what they did as well. It is also important to analyze whether you should have held onto a position longer or cut your losses quicker on a given position. If the stock started to go down, how quickly were you able to realize you were wrong and get out? What signals pointed you in this direction? By replaying the situations in your head you can get ready for what to do next time. It is also a good idea to look at other active stocks in the market. It is difficult to follow the whole market, but you can look for the most active stocks so that you can keep an eye out for them in the future.

What particular stocks or industries do you follow?

I really trade everything and anything that moves. I try and limit myself to not trading stocks under $5 unless there is something incredible going on, because my strategy is to look for extremely volatile stocks where the price can move a significant number of points in one day. As you get stocks that are cheaper in price, a one point movement is a larger overall percentage of their value—therefore they are less likely to make a significant jump in one day.

Why don't you just follow the Internet stocks?

A lot of traders just follow a certain industry, such as the Internet, but there is so much volatility in the market that there can be just as good of an opportunity in so many different industries. For example, I have done really well in the financial services industry over the last two years. You should not limit yourself to watching just one sector of the market when there is so much activity in so many different industries.

How do you watch so many stocks?

A lot of traders feel that you can realistically only cover 100 stocks. However, by working around other traders it is possible to cover hundreds more because you can pick up on pieces of information they are talking about and check out new stocks on your own. Also, at TRADESCAPE.*com* we use Tradescape Pro that allows you to see the most active movers on the day and keep track of news releases all on one screen.

How have you seen the opportunities change for electronic traders over the last two years?

The opportunities for electronic traders have skyrocketed. If you are making solely intra-day trades it is a little bit harder now, just because there are so many new traders. However, the opportunities to make money overall have gone up because of the increased volatility, which in turn creates more chances to make money. This also increases your risk, so it is especially important to be extra cautious when just starting out.

When you are just starting out how do you avoid not getting exploited by the more experienced traders and market makers?

The key is to start out slowly for the first couple of weeks by just watching the markets. The best way to prepare yourself is to use a training version of the trading software and pretend as if you were trading for real. Get into the habit of coming in before the markets open in the morning and staying after they close at night to prepare your strategy and review your trades.

How do you prepare yourself for the time it takes to become profitable?

Whatever money you plan on trading with, plan on losing 20 percent at the start. If you can not do this than you really should not get into trading solely intra day positions. You have to be able to risk the losses in order to make the really the big money.

What does it take, mentally, to be successful?

You really need to cut away from your emotions. The best traders are the ones that are like a machine—just buying and selling instinctively on their predetermined strategy and concentrating on making the right executions instead of their profits or losses. The hardest thing for a lot of traders to get over is the pride factor, especially when confidence is so important. When a stock is going down you need to be able to admit you were wrong and get out of the position immediately.

How do you control your risk?

I set a downside limit in terms of what I am willing to lose overall. For example, over a period of time such as a year, if I were to lose \$500,000 of a \$2,000,000 capital base, I would just just stop trading. In terms of in the middle of the day, if you lose money on three trades in a row, wait 20 minutes before you make another trade and sit and think about what you are doing wrong.

How do you take a step back mentally in the middle of the day when so much is going on?

You really don't have a choice if you want to have a career as a day trader. Discipline is so important. You hear about people not making it because they lack the discipline to regroup when things are not going their way. You are not always going to be in sync with the markets, however the key is recognizing when you are not, regrouping, and readjusting your strategy for the remainder of the day.

What does it take to make it as a successful day trader?

Discipline. Discipline to get over your fear of losing money and go for it when your analysis says you should be taking a large position. Discipline to sit there after the market closes for three hours and analyze your trades even after you made or lost \$70,000 over the course of the day.

What do you find are some of the misconceptions regarding electronic trading?

Everything talked about in Internet chat rooms. People take pieces of information about electronic trading and make it into something completely different. The problem is that there are so few people that actually understand what it is that there are an incredible number of misconceptions. Also, most of the media still has no idea of the difference between electronic trading and someone using E*TRADE.

How has electronic trading affected the financial industry as a whole?

By having traders access the markets directly, instead of through a middleman such as a market maker or broker, a lot of people are making a lot less commissions. The industry as a whole is really just emerging, because the original electronic trading firms kept a very low profile. At the time, they were on the verge of being disbanded, coupled with the fact that they had such a good thing going they did not want others to know about it. The general public is getting their first dose of electronic trading, however most individuals are still relatively uncomfortable with it because there is no one holding your hand during a trade, and there is so much more detailed analysis available.

How do you see the role of online investors affecting electronic trading?

Online investors are eventually going to really play a large part. All of the markets are steadily moving towards electronic trading and a more direct model. Other exchanges, such as the NYSE, are starting to update their trading systems and, eventually, everything will be traded electronically. If anything, online investors will propel the NYSE and all exchanges to promote electronic trading because it is more convenient and cost effective for them.

How would you describe your personal trading style?

I will always buy any stock if the movement is good. There are so many opportunities in the market it is crazy not to watch as much of what is going on as you can. The way to make the most money is really to look for all the opportunities, not just within a particular spot. When I see something that fits my criteria, I go for it.

How do you alter your strategy if you are not trading full time?

Before I decided I was going back to medical school, I used to trade at all times with 2/3 of my money in the market and keep 1/3 in reserve in cash. With that much of my personal wealth in the market in highly volatile stocks, I needed to be there, managing my positions full time as well as looking for new opportunities. When I decided to go back to medical school and would be trading part time, I liquidated all of my positions and bought less volatile stocks that I would not need to manage on a full time basis.

What sort of analysis do you use?

I essentially just analyze the movement of the stock. By watching the volume as the stock goes up and down I get a sense of when to buy or sell. I do not use any technical analysis. I do however memorize historical stock prices so that I have an idea if a stock is approaching an all time high or an all time low. This is extremely important because so many other people know these things as well and it is usually this psychology that will affect the stock price.

How often do you update your trading strategy?

I update my trading strategy almost daily. The marketplace changes so quickly now with the extremely high levels of volume that it forces you to re-examine your positions and overall strategy constantly.

What effects have ECNs had on electronic trading?

The advent of ECNs has created a lot of new opportunities for electronic traders. The most important aspect of ECNs is that they have increased overall liquidity for executing trades. As an electronic trader, you now have the option to make a trade using many different ECNs. The key is to know which one to use and when.

How do you know which ECN to use?

At TRADESCAPE.*com* we primarily use Island, however it depends on the firm or software you use. It really does not matter as long as you are on an ECN that has a lot of volume. There are a lot of other smaller ones that you want to avoid because they do not have a lot of volume and you may get stuck holding onto a trade because there is no buyer or seller. On the bigger ECNs, such as Island, you always have instantaneous execution.

What are the important things to look for in an electronic trading firm?

The most important things to look for are execution speed and quote speed. As an electronic trader, your edge is real-time access to news, quotes, and other market information. Even a split-second wait to receive a quote can result in the loss of hundreds or thousands of dollars. Another important factor is how willing other traders are to work with you. Get a feel for the environment and if they have any sort of training program. You can usually tell how good a firm is by how well their traders are doing.

How have you improved over the last two years?

Everyone can make money in an up market, but good day traders can make money in any market. Over the last two years, although we have been in a bull market overall, there have been numerous days when the market has crashed. These are the days that the good traders excel by shorting stocks and using their experience to know how the market reacts in situations such as these. Over the last two years I have learned how to trade in all types of market conditions, enabling me to frequently adjust my strategy and consistently make money.

Is it possible to trade other securities than just stocks on the NASDAQ?

You can already trade certain stocks on the NYSE using SuperDot, and they are considering electronic trading for other securities as well such as options. It would be only natural for everything to move towards more of a direct model. We will also see a lot more activity overseas with electronic trading over the next couple of years.

What do you see as the future of electronic trading if the market crashes?

If the market crashes, electronic traders can actually make a ton of money. That is the best thing about being an electronic trader—the versatility. Electronic traders are actually the most poised to take advantage of a market crash. In the long run, a market crash is not good for anyone. However, usually market crashes are followed by a lot of activity which electronic traders thrive on.

What has electronic trading taught you?

It has been a great experience. I made a lot of money and had a lot of fun. What I learned is that money does not matter as long as you are doing something you really enjoy. There are so many people making so little money and working extremely hard doing something they do not enjoy. The key is to do something you really love and have a passion for—you will usually be successful and make money at it.

13

THE WINNING PSYCHE

—Sohail Khalid

SOHAIL KHALID JUMPED OFF THE TYPICAL FINANCIAL TRACK, WHICH WOULD HAVE LED HIM INTO INVESTMENT BANKING OR CONSULTING, TO HELP HIS COUSIN START AN ELECTRONIC TRADING FIRM SEVERAL YEARS AGO. SOHAIL BELIEVES THAT HIS TRADING EDGE COMES FROM UNDERSTANDING THE PUBLIC PSYCHE, HOW IT REACTS TO AND MOVES THE MARKETS. HIS SUCCESS IS ALMOST ENTIRELY ATTRIBUTABLE TO THE GREAT VALUE HE PLACES ON PREPARATION; HE RESPECTS AND FEARS THE MARKET AND USES HIS KNOWL-EDGE OF IT BOTH TO ANTICIPATE LIKELY MOVEMENTS AND TO EXPECT THE UNEXPECTED.

How did you become involved in day trading?

Traditionally, to become a professional trader at a Wall Street firm, one had to undertake a long, sometimes arduous process of being a trader's assistant for a period of at least two to three years. While still in college I began to develop an interest in what was at the time a fairly new phenomenon, day trading. I thought of day trading as a way to cut through the conventional bureaucracy in the professional trading world. I viewed this as an opportunity to almost immediately begin executing my own trades for my own account.

How did you develop your skills as an electronic trader without previous trading experience?

Before I began, I took some time to study the nature of the market. I felt it was very important to learn from other experienced traders. I read books such as Market Wizards, New Market Wizards, and Reminiscence of a Stock Operator-these were helpful in giving me some insight on different perspectives from professionals in the business.

How quickly did you develop into a successful trader?

After about five or six months of studying, again mainly from reading and observation, I was fortunate enough to be profitable after just my first month of 'live' trading. After my second month I was the most profitable trader in my firm. I think the key behind that was that I rarely focused on how much money I was making, but rather I focused on what I was doing to make profitable trades.

What was the strategy that made you so successful?

My strategy was not to go for the big money right away. Instead, I first focused on developing the fundamentals. As the saying goes, one must first learn to crawl before one can walk. This holds true for anything you do in life. For example, a professional athlete must go through years of intense training before becoming skilled in his sport.

I was very careful not to rush my training process. I have seen many new faces enter the profession in haste, and leave shortly after. An important thing to remember is that the market is not going anywhere. It's been around for decades, and it will be around for years to come.

How important is psyche in electronic trading?

A traders psyche or state of mind is one of the most important elements in defining a successful trader. If a trader loses his edge, or loses control of his emotions, he puts himself at a great disadvantage. This I learned at a very early stage of my career. When emotion comes into the picture your whole rational changes, you will find yourself executing trades not based on logic, or what a stock should do, but rather what you want the stock to do. One of the hardest lessons one has to learn is that he cannot simply will the market to act as he sees fit. Instead of trying to create the waves, a successful trader will consistently ride the waves that already exist.

The stock market is comprised of thousands of traders exchanging almost a billion shares a day. I don't believe the market fluctuates the way it does due to a series of irrelevant buy or sell orders. The market takes on the personality of those who trade it. That is why I spend a considerable amount of time to try to understand the personality of the market, which seems to change from day to day.

What are some of the trading rules you live by?

It is very important to stick to the fundamentals, the very basic steps of how to make profitable trades. For me such things as recognizing an ideal buying situation, recongnizing when to offer stock, and realizing when to sell the stock on the bid are very basic, but can prove to be very effective for consistency. Another very important aspect of this is keeping your emotions in check. Because you are dealing with money, it's only natural to get emotionally involved. No matter how fundamentally sound you are, you cannot be effective if your mind takes a backseat to your emotions. For this reason exactly I try very hard not to think of the dollars and cents until after the closing bell.

How do you handle making losing trades or mental errors?

There are times when you can make the right decision yet still lose money on the trade. Because there are no set rules for how the market is supposed to act, there is no definitive right or wrong. The best a trader can do is act within the parameters of what he believes is the right trade. So for me it didn't bother me so much if I lost money on a trade as long as I executed what I felt was the right trade. This again leads back to ones emotions. I realized it was very important to learn how to deal with mistakes and learn from them rather than let them consume your thoughts. It's meaningful to remember exactly what you did wrong, and it's essential to take lessons from your mistakes.

How do you keep your strategy updated over time?

Consider the fact that the market is changing every day. It is a different animal then it was a decade ago, a year ago, or even a month ago. I think it's vital to keep in touch with some of the underlying factors that make up this change, such as an increasing number of personalities, more money, and better technology. Therefore I have found it necessary to be flexible. I have seen others who were successful in the past but were so set in their ways that would eventually lose out because they were unable and unwilling to cope with change. The market tends to move in phases where different sectors are more active than others. I think it is important to recognize this and of course, take advantage of it.

How do you stay on top of your game and maintain your edge?

The key ingredient here is preparation. In such a volatile and unpredictable market, you must always prepare yourself for the unexpected. If you never make assumptions, you will never be caught off-guard. Traders who are able to prepare themselves mentally for different situations are able to capitalize on opportunities that exist in the market in the most effective manner possible. This is what sets the top tier of traders apart from everyone else. Each experience you have during your career should be used to enhance your overall understanding to give you more insight into the market.

What has trading taught you?

I have found there to be a very strong correlation between my trading life and my personal life. I have learned to place a large emphasis on preparation, whereas when I was younger I may have rushed into situations prematuraly. I also feel trading has taught me to mature emotionally on many levels. I feel trading has forced me to be a much more controlled person than I was before I started trading.

What can you learn from other electronic traders?

I have learned some very valuable lessons from other traders. Having a camaraderie and being able to share your experiences with other skilled traders plays a critical role in ones development. I try to find strengths in other traders and incorporate them within myself.

What is the most important aspect of succeeding in this business?

If you want to make trading your career, you had better be sure you love something about it, because it takes a very driven person to really succeed. In my opinion, if you are not somewhat passionate about what you are doing you will have a very hard time sticking with it during the hard times. Because it has a steep learning curve, trading is a profession where you can be discouraged very easily if you are not fully dedicated. Most importantly for me is that I had a very strong determination, which I relentlessly pursued in order to be among the best.

Is there any way that computers could replace electronic traders?

Machines or computers will never be able to outperform humans because they lack one key ingredient, intuition.

Intuition is the key for all traders, and it is what sets one trader apart from another. When given the opportunity to observe the market, the human mind has an unbelievable capacity to comprehend and digest what it sees. This understanding and knowledge has to be almost innate so that you can react instantaneously to opportunities presented to you. This is why a good trader can understand something fully without ever being able to explain it. I am rarely able to explain what I see in the market, yet I am able to make extremely accurate trades that I attribute to intuition.

What sets one trader apart from another?

Just that "intuition." It is the major difference between traders. Two traders can be sitting next to each other and looking at the same information, yet one is going to notice something faster and more accurately than the other. Many times there will be a certain piece of information which will trigger his mind before the other guy and make all the difference in capitalizing on the trade. The elite traders do not really even have to think about what they are doing; it is all instinctively driven by intuition. After only a few short minutes of observation, I can get a pretty good feel for the market on any given day.

How long will electronic trading be a good opportunity?

We are certainly only at the early stages of electronic trading. Electronic trading was an infant ten years ago, so by that measure it is still a child today. As interest continues to grow and technology continues to develop, the stock market will proceed to grow at a very rapid pace. There was a time when the top professions were doctors, engineers, lawyers, etc... We are not too far away from the trading profession being considered as a fundamentally sound and highly recommended career.

14

SURVIVING AS AN ELECTRONIC TRADER

—*David Kuang*

D AVID KUANG HAS BEEN DAY TRADING SINCE DECEMBER 1996 AFTER
LEAVING HIS POST-COLLEGE CONSULTING JOB. ACCORDING TO DAVID, THE
KEY TO BEING A SUCCESSFUL DAY TRADER IS SURVIVAL, BY MEANS OF NOT ONLY
HARD WORK, BUT ALSO PERSONAL AS WELL AS FINANCIAL VISION AND SELF-
AWARENESS. ELECTRONIC TRADING HAS BEEN A MEANS TO AN END FOR DAVID.
HE IS NOW STARTING UP HIS OWN BUSINESS WITH THE CAPITAL HE ACCRUED
FROM HIS YEARS AS A FULL-TIME TRADER.

How did you get started in electronic trading?

I started back in December 1996. I'd been interested in the
stock market throughout college, and I had been working as a
consultant for a couple of years after graduation. I realized
that I didn't like the corporate politics involved in consulting,

159

and also that trading was the one way that I could make a lot of money really fast. I had a friend in New York who worked at the trading desk of Smith Barney who mentioned a small electronic trading company in New York that was doing really well. I didn't know what electronic trading was at the time, but I was happy to get any trading job.

How much financial experience had you had before you started trading?

I had a finance background from MIT, but the funny thing is, I think I knew too much. I think a lot of people have the misconception that day trading is really a complicated science, but right off the bat, the firm preached to it's members that it's simply momentum trading.

What was a typical day like for you when you first started trading?

The first day I came in I was assigned to apprentice with one of the veteran traders, who happened to be this crazy trader who only spoke what sounded like gibberaish. I watched the traders for two days before I started getting involved, but on my very first day of trading, the market was going down in a hurry. I didn't know what was going on, but my trainer kept telling me, "David, get short!" Get short what? What's short? I had no idea what short was, much less that it was the only way to make money when the market was going down. He told me to get into market stocks, and started rattling off the ticker symbols of stocks. I had no idea what he was talking about. I told him that I couldn't get short, so he said, "Well, hit a high bid!" But there were no high bids. And then, all of a sudden, I started to see them pop up—"There's one! There's another one! Should I hit 'em?" I asked. And he said, "Hit 'em!" So I got short. But where do you see high bids when the market goes down? At the bottom. So I ended up being short about 2,000 share—which was a lot, especially for my first day—in all these market stocks at the bottom of the market. And all at once they started going up. My trainer yelled at me, "Cover!" and I said, "What do you mean, 'cover'?" He wanted me to buy them back, but I had no idea how to buy them back. Most traders, when they start out, trade only a couple hundred shares a day: my first day I traded 76,000 shares. My second day I traded even more. I was miserable. I came in thinking it was easy money, and already I had hit bottom. I should have been on a simulator and any electronic trading company now would never let that happen.

What was it that turned it around for you?

When I realized that my trainer didn't know what he was talking about. But that was a very rough awakening. I didn't stop losing money until my third month. I finally met this person, whom I'd gone to school with, who was trading at the desk right in front of me. I could watch him pretty easily, and he would consistently make money every single day. I talked to him a lot, and he explained to me how to go for the easy money, not necessarily the big money, but taught me that I needed to walk before I could run. That's when I realized that this job wasn't as easy as I'd thought it was going to be—at that point, I didn't even need to make a ton of money, I just wanted to survive. I always pass that wisdom on to new traders: the key to success is first learning how to survive. It is such a tough market that if you get too cocky and take too many risks, you're going to go belly up fairly quickly. It doesn't hurt to lose money as long as you learn, but make sure you learn.

**How was it that you are now able to make those
consistent gains? What is your survival strategy?**

When a stock was going down, people would panic and hit the
bids through the market—we called that "buying a stock
through" or "buy-throughs." What we would do, when stocks
were going down, was look for the ones that were going down
very fast and put in bids that were below the market. We
would try this about 20 times during the day. Maybe three of
those times a market maker would hit our bid through the
market because they had a customer who was panicking and
really wanted to sell, and then we would just turn around and
sell it immediately at the current bid and make a little bit of
money. That's how I first began to survive.

**If you had to start all over again in today's
market, how would your strategy have been
different?**

I've been training a woman who's now consistently making
$2,000-$3,000 a day doing some very conservative trading.
The way she's doing it is by finding small stocks that have
been oversold at the open. At the open there are often imbalances between the buy and sell orders that beat the market
inefficiencies, which basically means that you can often find
$5, $10, $15 stocks that have been oversold by a point. So if
you can look for that bottom, you'll sometimes be able to buy
that stock on the bid in the morning. When the orders balance out, the stock will drift up half a point, so you can make
$500 on 1,000 shares of stock. Do that two or three times a
day, and you're in good shape. The way to start is to learn
how to work with small stocks and buy them on the bid,
where they really can't go too far against you, and you're in
a low-risk situation.

It sounds like every trader needs to have a two-month period where he needs to learn the ropes and expect to take losses. Once you're consistently making money, what's the next step in terms of stepping your trading up a notch?

There are so many levels, but the next level up from the most basic is an increase in size. If you're trading a stock in 1,000-share increments and finding that you're successful, you'll want to start trading in 2,000-share blocks. Once you've figured out how to make high probability trades, you want to be able to maximize that trade. What you don't want to have to do yet is branch into another area of trading with a lower probability. You have to find the area of trading that has the highest probability of success and max it out before you go on to the area with the next-highest probability of success. You just keep on doing that until you max out all the potential.

As a beginner, what types of stocks should someone be looking for?

In the beginning, you want to stay away from highly active stocks, simply because of the nature of those stocks. With all the orders being placed and bids coming in, active stocks can very easily panic a young trader. The key to learning the fundamentals is in the thinly traded, widespread stocks. You always want to try to be the big fish in a small pond. If you play these thinly traded small stocks, even as a novice electronic trader you are still a big player. Beginners need to think about the fact that if they're in the big stocks, they're competing with the experts—guys like Kirk Kazazian and David Lu.

**With the new ECNs and all the different methods
of execution, how do traders know which ones
they should use?**

That's tantamount to the real issue, which is: "How do you
determine when a stock's been oversold or overbought?"
That's the real question that beginners need to ask themselves, not "What is the best means of buying or selling a
stock?" If a stock is oversold by half a point, it doesn't matter
how you buy it, as long as you buy it.

**How important is it to be able to react
instinctively to a situation?**

You've got to visualize. One day I was watching Netscape, and
saw that it was going up and up and up. I didn't play it that
day, but I knew that the next day, there was going to be a ton
of money in the stock. I didn't sleep a wink that night because
I was dreaming about all the scenarios I could exploit with
that stock! The next morning I came in and made a lot of
money in only 20 minutes. It was all about visualization. The
only reason people don't react instinctively is because they're
not prepared to have to do that—they're not trained. It's
important to have foresight and to imagine all the possible
situations that could occur once you've purchased a stock: if 'A'
happens, what do I do? If 'B' happens, if 'C' happens? A lot of
traders get caught up in *"Am I in the money or am I out of the
money?"* It's very important to visualize the potential scenarios so that not only can you react mentally but also physical-
ly—your fingers need to fly across the keyboard.

**You said before that there were certain things in
the movement of a stock that tipped you off—**

what are those things? Is it the volume, the way it spikes, historical levels—or can you even quantify it?

I see the signals on several levels, but I boil everything down to one simple question: Is this stock overbought or oversold? If the answer is "yes" to either option, I know that there's profit potential. I look for continuous buying or panic in the market. The only way that you can get a feel for that is watching the stock over time. For example, the trading room around you will often give you a feel for what's going on: If the traders are all freaking out about the fact that they can't buy a certain stock, I know that that's indicative of how the market is responding as a whole. The volume can tell you whether or not it's active, but the telltale sign of a stock's profit potential is its volatility—how fast the stock is moving. As long as I see rapid movement, I know that a stock can be overbought or oversold more easily, and therefore, there's more profit potential.

Do you use any fundamental or technical analyses on a regular basis?

I use a lot of technical analyses. Whenever I think about trading a stock, I always check out a historical daily chart. I find out where the areas of support and resistance are; I look for an intra-day analysis so that I can see how rapidly a stock is moving in how short a period of time. I always check how liquid a stock is, especially how many shares outstanding it has, because an absolutely normal stock can do amazing things when the float is very small. I also keep an eye on the news, but I don't try to analyze it—I just want to know why people are buying or selling.

How do you use the other traders around you?

I think there's a lot of value to be gained from trading on an electronic trading floor—especially when you first start out; this can be your greatest asset. A novice trader has to be hypersensitive to what other people are doing, because that's where you learn a lot about electronic trading. One day, we were all trading this stock that went up tremendously fast. I ended up losing a lot of money in five minutes in this stock. The trader next to me had lost a lot as well and was sitting at his desk hyperventilating. Everybody was yelling at each other. I'd only been trading for about six months, and I'd just about wiped out my account; I was scrambling desperately to get back. Then, through the grapevine, I started hearing about all these other expert traders who are going long in the stock—20,000 and 40,000 shares each—and everybody else on the floor who's hearing this is trying to copy them. I knew that I immediately had to sell off my position. Because if all these great traders are going long in a stock—they'd bought all the stock they'd wanted to buy and it *still* hadn't gone up—then there must be some serious sellers out there. If the best traders in the world had bought all that stock and it still hadn't gone up, then it must be going down. Momentum trading is fine, but you should never chase a stock. What beginners need to learn in the first three to six months is how to determine when momentum is slowing down, because that inevitably precedes the top or the bottom of a move. It's imperative to get out of your stock before there's no longer the demand for it.

Do you do any market analysis before or after market hours?

When I first started out, I came in an hour and a half before the open and stayed an hour after the close of the market. This is one of the best times to check out what's happened the previous day and to make your projections and start to visu-

alize about the day ahead. I recommend that every new trader keep a notebook and record all the stocks that they've
either played or were of interest to them. For each stock, they
should write down their own personal analysis: What stock
did I buy? Did I make money in it? How could I have made
more money in it? Be very constructive when you evaluate
your moves—sometimes you can learn more from evaluating
the good trades than from evaluating the bad. You're always
going to have bad trades. The key is to figure out how to make
more good trades, and how to max out those good trades.
When you open up a trade, you go long, and you expose yourself to risk, so you're often very quick to take a profit. When
you're out of the money in a stock, you're not so quick to take
a loss, because you don't want to lose money. Its very important to look back on a successful trade and ask yourself, "How
could I have made more money in this stock?"

How do you mitigate your risk in terms of setting
a good risk model for yourself from the start?

The key to being successful from the start is developing discipline. The way that I used to measure risk reward was on a
sheet of paper, before I would buy a stock, I would determine
how much I was risking for the potential return. I would try
to get a feel for how much risk I was taking on for my level of
trading. The key to mitigating your risk is to know your own
capabilities—in terms of capital, in terms of ability to cut
losses. I've heard people say that you should never have more
than 2 percent of the assets in one stock at a time, and that
you should never risk more than an eighth, but that's not the
correct philosophy if you want to make a lot of money. It's all
about risk reward. I'll risk five points to make 20 points, or
$5,000 to make $20,000. What separates the great traders
from the rest is the confidence with which they evaluate risk.
If you write down your risk reward evaluation every time, you

start to have more confidence in your trades, and you become a better trader.

How has your trading philosophy evolved over time?

The most important thing to do is to find your "edge" in electronic trading. In order to be the best trader that I can be, I have to know what my edge is. For me, it might be my speed of execution; for someone else, it might be his analytical skills. Every electronic trader is different.

How do you see electronic trading evolving?

I think there's more money in the market now than there ever was before—there are more people in it, there's more liquidity. Before, electronic traders used to make money off of market makers in the small, volatility stocks. Now, with so many people trading in the market, the profitability of small moves is slowly disappearing. I think that the really big money comes when the institutions step in and there's a really big price move. The stock ends up getting overbought or oversold, and there's so much liquidity in the market that you can get a very big position—30,000 or 40,000 shares—in the stock for two or three points. So what I would say is that the opportunities come less frequently, but when they do, they're huge.

How do you see the smaller online investors affecting the market as a whole?

I think it's good for the market because the more liquidity you have in the market, the better. Having investors gambling in the marketplace, however, is bad. It changes the whole mentality and structure of the market. It has serious side effects. Alan Greenspan, Chairman of the Federal Reserve, has referred to the Internet as a lottery system, and in a way it is: you risk a small amount of money to have your stock split five times and go up 600 percent. In the end though, I think online investors will be beneficial.

Do you see a lot of individuals who are currently trading online making the move to electronic trading, where they have direct access to the markets?

What I do see is that everyone wants that kind of information. Once it is made readily available to the market, there's going to be a huge demand for it. The only barrier is going to be the learning curve—it's a little scary. Traders who ask a lot of questions and prepare themselves well before they start using it will realize success, because they will have the access to the most accurate and most current information.

Do you think that we're moving toward a market where people will be able to trade other things than just stocks on the NASDAQ?

Yes and no: yes because I've already seen it occurring with futures and the like, and no because there's no edge in doing it. Those markets, like futures, have access to a floor where you have to go through a broker anyway. The real edge of electronic trading is that we can execute more quickly than market makers and don't have to rely on anyone else. I have a friend who's a broker at Merrill Lynch, and the system that he uses is 10 times slower than mine—I've already finished making a trade by the time he types in his order and the quote comes up. Even though electronic trading in other securities will evolve, there's not a real edge there yet. There's no point in getting involved in that until order execution has been automated.

Is there any way to day trade on a part-time basis?

People have to realize that this is the most competitive opportunity in the world. If you're not willing to dedicate the necessary time and effort—not as a get-rich-quick scheme and not as a hobby, but as a full-time profession—you can't expect to succeed. When you're very serious and very focused and you've spent a lot of time in the electronic trading world, you can start to back away and still make money. Everyone's end goals for day trading are different: some people want the thrill, other people are in it for wealth, and for others, it's a stepping stone. But the common denominator for everyone who's been successful is simple: hard work.

What do you think electronic trading has taught you?

Perhaps, most obviously, electronic trading has taught me that success does not come easily. I can tell you that I've almost wiped out my account now about four or five times, and every time I do, it's a real emotional battle to come back and sit down at the terminal again. I've been lucky; I was able to take advantage of the opportunities when they came around. Trading has also taught me a lot about self-discipline: some of the best traders are so self-disciplined that you can't tell anything about their bank accounts by talking to them—you can never tell whether they're up or down. I'm nowhere near that stoic, but I have learned a lot about self-control.

Do you see yourself doing this for a long time?

I'm actually using electronic trading as a stepping stone. I'm using it to build wealth so that I have enough capital to start my own business, which I'm currently doing right now. I still trade, but only part time. I don't think that trading is what's right for me long term, but everyone has to evaluate his own individual situation.

How do you know if it's not for you?

I think that if you try it for three to six months and you're still not having fun, then it's probably not for you. If you're not content with how you're progressing, or you just can't see the light at the end of the tunnel, then maybe it's time to find something else. I came into trading saying that I wanted to make six figures my first year, and I wanted to make a million dollars in seven years—little did I know that I'd be doing it a year and a half into my trading career. If you don't have that drive or vision, then maybe it's not for you.

Any parting words of advice that you would give to someone just starting off in day trading?

Have fun. Electronic trading has so many highs and lows that it's easy to get caught up in the roller coaster, but you've got to make sure that you're having fun on the ride. It's an opportunity that very few people have the option to pursue, so if that's what interests you and you can afford to do it, don't let it pass you by.

15

THE FUTURE OF ELECTRONIC TRADING

—Omar Amanat

O MAR AMANAT FELT THE UNMISTAKABLE RUSH THE VERY FIRST TIME HE TRADED ELECTRONICALLY. HE BOUGHT SHARES FROM TRADERS AT MERRILL LYNCH. HE SOLD SHARES TO TRADERS AT GOLDMAN SACHS. HE WAS 22 YEARS OLD, HE WAS TRADING WITH THE TOP PROFESSIONALS IN THE WORLD, AND HE WAS MAKING MONEY. HE SAW FELLOW DAY TRADERS MAKE TENS OF THOUSANDS OF DOLLARS IN PROFIT IN A MATTER OF MINUTES. HE FELT AN ELECTRICITY WITH EACH AND EVERY NEW TRADE AND EACH NEW OPPORTUNITY. HE WOULD DREAM ABOUT IT AT NIGHT. HE WOULD ALSO HAVE NIGHTMARES ABOUT PLACING HUNDREDS OF THOUSANDS OF DOLLARS ON THE WRONG STOCK. MOST OF ALL, HE WOULD GO TO WORK THE NEXT DAY AND SEE THAT THIS WAS NO FANTASY. HE WAS IN THE MARKET IN REAL-TIME, WHEN SO MUCH OF THE REST OF THE WORLD WOULDN'T KNOW WHAT WAS HAPPENING UNTIL THEY READ IT IN TOMORROW'S PAPER, AND THE OPPORTUNITIES WERE VERY REAL.

There was a certain power in being able to submit an order and directly deal with firms such as Merrill Lynch, or Goldman Sachs. I put in an order just like I did every day, and my execution would read, "You bought 200 shares from Merrill Lynch." It was just such an empowering feeling, knowing I was really on the same level with such established companies.

In fact, it felt as though I had too much of an advantage. The market makers had systems that were clearly too slow. These lumbering institutions were too slow to react to my moves.

A short time before, Amanat was one of those traders using the old-fashioned system. Trading derivatives at Citibank, Amanat had a phone that kept him in constant touch with other dealers, printed price lists—that quickly became outdated—and the shouts of other Citibank traders as they announced prices at which they bought and sold, or what they had available to trade. In that situation, no one could be precisely sure what prices should be from one moment to the next. This was the inefficiency in the market that Amanat would arbitrage when he began day trading. A stock could start to move up, but not every market maker would be as swift to recognize the move and adjust prices before Amanat and his electronic connection could swoop in and grab 1,000 shares at the old low price. Now he could resell those shares for an instant profit, or hold, if he saw that the price was continuing to climb and some market makers were still in a scramble to play catch up.

So our fear back then was: What happens when the market makers begin to replace their antiquated systems? What happens when more people start day trading? The market would get more efficient and the opportunities we had would begin to disappear. Then what were we going to do?

What ended up happening, actually, was the reverse. The volume of trading has so expanded that there are more opportunities than ever. That doesn't mean that it's less risk. It's just as risky as it always was, but with so many more opportunities to trade and much more money that can be made.

Perhaps the biggest irony in all this is that technology first developed for day trading has been refined and expand-

ed and led to the creation of today's Electronic
Communication Networks (ECNs), an advance in investment
market technology that is making markets more efficient,
more fair and more powerful. The day trading technology once
heavily criticized by the Wall Street establishment—even
reviled—as meddling with the ability of market makers to set
prices and maintain markets for conventional investors, is
benefiting individuals and institutions alike by cutting the
time and money required to make trades. The momentum to
provide after-hours trading, so investors can make trades
when it is convenient for them instead of when it is convenient for Wall Street brokers, is due in large part to the ease
with which ECNs can facilitate this trading.

Day traders helped push the envelope of technology in
the market and the resulting efficiencies have expanded the
market and expanded opportunities in the classic style that
technology helps economies transform and grow: cutting out
steps in the process, cutting time, boosting efficiency and cutting the cost of doing business significantly enough that a
whole new level of demand is unleashed in the marketplace,
and with it, opportunities no forecaster could have dared to
predict. That is the power of the Internet and the information
economy, which has so astounded many conventional
investors and economists. It is a classic example of a para-
digm shift. Technology developed for some other purpose
begins to take on a life of its own, unleashing creative forces
and a wave of changes that ultimately turn an industry on its
head.

There may in fact be no better example of the overall
scope of this opportunity than Amanat himself, who at 26 is
chief executive officer of Tradescape.com, a company serving
day traders with the most advanced technology for electronic
investing and direct connections with the markets, ECNs and
other sources of liquidity. How does he compare the chal-
lenges of being CEO of one of the biggest and fastest growing
companies in his industry to those of day trading? There are
remarkable similarities, he says. Skills he honed as a trader

he uses everyday as an executive: the ability to make decisions rapidly and unemotionally, to recognize key trends as they develop, the understanding that it's important to cut losses quickly in order to keep your focus and your resources on areas of maximum opportunity.

In the following pages, Omar Amanat provides some perspective on the day trading phenomenon and reflections on the new products, services and opportunities that will be available to day traders and other investors because of the shift in market power that has occurred.

First and foremost, to understand how the future of day trading and electronic trading may unfold, you have to understand that this is a technology trend. In a business enabled by technology that didn't exist until a very few years ago, growth is likely to evolve following patterns of development we have seen repeatedly with other technology products and services. That is: speed and power increase exponentially, all the while the price comes down and the product becomes simpler and simpler to use. The market doesn't just grow incrementally, it appears to explode, because there is not just one factor encouraging growth, but everything that could possibly figure into the demand equation. For comparison, think of demand for new home construction. It is fed by population growth, with up and down cycles related to employment and interest rate conditions. In a really good year there might be 10 percent growth. Now imagine that new homes could be built twice as big, for half the price, and never needed painting. That's what happens when technology transforms a business.

Investing with direct electronic access is a classic technology killer app. It doesn't simply replace old technology. Like some other killer apps—the fax, or Federal Express or the cellular phone—it lets us do things we never could do before and creates new demand from new customers. A whole new industry is built seemingly out of thin air. In reality, the market was there all along. People wanted to do it; there just wasn't any way they could. But today, individuals can have the virtual equivalent of a seat on the stock exchange. Today they can bypass their broker and the trader and the market maker, who would have all had to help handle their trade in the past, and they can personally place their order in the market to be filled.

Seeing this business through the eyes of a technologist makes it clear that once one of these new markets appears, there are waves and waves of technological innovation to come that continue to drive the growth of the business. Though experts may tell us that the niche market with the exploding growth will soon be saturated, the reality is that the pace of technological improvement can enable the business to begin reaching beyond a mainstream audience. And with a potential customer base tens or hundreds of times greater, the growth only accelerates. Then spinoff applications from the proven technology or service drive growth even farther and even faster.

So what are some of these technology trends, already in use in other businesses or ready to come off the drawing boards, that will be showing up in the months and years ahead for use by day traders and a wide range of other investors?

Smart systems: Like a staff of assistants and analysts watching the market for you, a beep, a page or a color coded chart will tell you exactly when something happens that you may want to act on. And with wireless systems and powerful handheld devices, you'll be able to follow the markets as closely from a chair at a sunny beach as an investor 10 years ago who was on the floor of the exchange.

Personalization: This is one of the hot buzzwords of e-commerce and one of the distinct competitive advantages of Internet businesses, where your news page can be a one-of-a-kind publication featuring headlines about your biggest investments, scores, and features only for your favorite teams. What Amazon.com can do by analyzing your purchase patterns and asking a few questions, can also be applied to investors. Imagine a system that understands your investment style and is able to recommend stocks—from anywhere in the world—that exhibit similar traits. This system may be able to make suggestions for logical diversification moves that would be ideal comple-ments to the investments you have. Or it may be able to help you identify specific characteristics of investments that have been your most successful and generate a list of stocks that seem to match those select criteria.

Internet business model: We're giving away as much information for free as we can, because that's the value-added proposition on the Internet. Providing more and more content and ever more powerful tools gives cus-tomers discretion and control over how they wish to use a product or service. This ability to control the experience is a large part of what truly empowers investors and defines the Internet age as completely distinct from the old industrial age, where the mantra was efficiency through mass production (or mass bureaucracy) and the corollary was one size fits all.

Simplify: The greatest and most widely used technol-ogy is often the simplest to use. Sophisticated and com-plex routines are all in the background, where the experts can monitor and maintain them. The user does-n't have to concern himself. That makes the technology all the more powerful, because everyone can use it, every-one has access. The telephone is a perfect example. For investors, that means that there will be nothing intimi-dating about applying the most advanced technology ever created to manage their investments. It will be easy to use, low cost, as well as powerful and effective.

As promising and powerful as the technology trends underly-ing the day trading revolution are, some similarly significant forces in the investment markets can contribute to continued growth of advanced electronic trading and direct market access.

However, many of you have probably heard just the opposite. In fact, you might be shocked to hear me say such a thing. "Day trading is just a speculative fad," or "day trading is no different than gambling," or "day traders will disappear in the next bear market," are all statements I hear every day. I often hear them from people with degrees and credentials that suggest the speaker has tremendous experience and insight into the workings of financial markets. Indeed, these are people who understand quite a lot about how financial markets have worked over the last 20, 30, or 40 years, but in this case that big-picture perspective betrays them. They see behavior that they have seen before—rapid-fire, aggressive, generating spectacular, almost unheard of, short-term returns—and when they have seen it before they have often seen it end badly. They do not look below the surface in this case to realize that new technology and new market rules have changed the game.

Let's start by talking about what will happen to day traders in the next bear market, or if there should be a dramatic crash, such as in October 1987. Initially, a classic day trader who buys and sells throughout the day, but ends each day holding little or no stock overnight, will probably start out miles ahead. If the decline is kicked off in dramatic fashion by some bit of news, a new and unsettling economic report, turmoil in an overseas market, for instance—these things traditionally happen when the market is closed and the result is that prices begin trading with an immediate drop of 2 percent, 3 percent, or 10 percent in the crash scenario.

So far, so good. Now what? Undoubtedly the market will be nervous and volatile. Investors may be tempted to look for bargains. But they will be wary that if there is another shoe to drop, the declines could be even more dramatic than in the first wave of selling. This will be a difficult market for all investors. Day traders will be in the same boat as all investors.

In such a market, investors will be understandably reluctant to make any significant commitments. While trading will likely be heavy, liquidity will probably be strained. The distinction here is that on a normal day there might be investors who would be willing to buy millions upon millions of shares of Microsoft if the price were to dip 1/4 or 1/2. The level of uncertainty on this day means that the price moves required to bring buyers and sellers together in sufficient quantity could range up and down over many dollars per share. The day trading methodology depends on liquidity so that the trader can execute his buy and sell orders. In a market situation where small bouts of buying and selling push stocks quickly over a wide range of prices, a day trader will encounter difficulty establishing desired positions even at those moments when they see an opportunity.

For example, in a broad based market decline, day traders can use short selling to profit from the decline. But not easily when stock prices might be moving downward in gulps of several dollars per share, and pausing only briefly at various levels before dropping anew. There will be a lot of competition to get whatever shares are available for short selling, and there will be a limited amount of time to establish any short positions at each price level.

Still, day traders are accustomed to identifying and working with trends. The argument that they won't recognize or know how to respond to a bear market strikes me as hilariously naïve, since day traders see bull and bear markets in microcosm each day with the fluctuations in markets and individual stocks. With the technology at their disposal, the day trader will be in a better position than most to assess the minute-by-minute shifts in market mood and be positioned accordingly.

What we've been talking about is an extreme situation. What about more normal market environments? Do day traders and day trading strategies have some elements investors can rely on to give them a persistent edge? I think the answer is yes, and the answer goes to the heart of the way the game has changed completely in just the past few years.

The day trader's advantages are information and speed, classic competitive weapons, and hardly the tricks of rogues or speculators. Thanks to regulatory changes designed to make markets more open and fair for all participants, we can see the buy and sell orders in the market with Level-2 NASDAQ quotes. We can see whether the orders are building up to push a stock price higher or lower. We can watch the behavior of key market makers for quirks that might signal that an important shift in the direction of a stock may be about to occur. Then we can react to that faster than many brokers or institutions who are trying to trade tens of thousands or hundreds of thousands of shares.

Looking back 10 or 20 years, it is clear that individual investors used to start out about three giant steps behind the pros on Wall Street. They didn't have access to the latest market news or investment research. When they bought a stock they would likely pay a fraction more than many of the institutions buying the same stock at the same time, and when they sold, their price would be lower by a similar amount. To top it all off, they paid the highest commissions for their transactions. With all of those things working against them, the only sensible strategy available to individuals was to take the slow and steady approach. If they paid a few dollars more for each investment, but held the investment for 10 years, then their initial disadvantage could be reduced to a more palatable level of a few cents per year.

On the basis of that history, generations of financial planners, authors and other experts intoned that individuals should buy and hold, and that any other investment technique must, by definition, be flawed from the start.

Simply put, many of the fears about day trading rest on assumptions that were overdue for re-examination. Throughout history, trading has proven to be quite lucrative. Many of the most venerable names on Wall Street were built with trading profits. What makes the best traders is the access to the best information and the best and lowest-cost systems for executing trades. Now those secrets are out.

Trading profits can't be hoarded by members of an exclusive club any longer.

There is yet another area where I have heard people express doubts about whether day trading is here to stay and whether it can continue its rapid growth. This, too, appears to be based at least in part on a misjudgment about the sophistication of day trading techniques and strategies, as well as a misunderstanding of the trends that have fueled the growth of day trading over the past few years.

We've discussed how technology is key to the trend, and that more powerful technology is always on the way. We've discussed how we are in the early stages of individuals being able to take advantage of the opportunities that have always been there for professionals inside Wall Street firms.

So what about the concern that day trading has only flourished because of the Internet stock boom. I suppose it's a natural assumption, because day trading has exploded at just about exactly the same time as the Internet stock frenzy. But the truth is that day traders are not as dependent on these particular fast-moving, high-flying stocks as many people believe. On any given day, there can be quite a few stocks from other sectors that command the attention of many day traders. Plus, the Internet stock boom really illustrates something much more basic and fundamental about markets and human nature. That is the tendency to focus particular attention and excitement in some group of stocks or industry sector. It may be an area where dynamic changes are occurring. It may be an area that was overlooked for a long period of time and has suddenly come back into favor as part of the periodic sector and style rotations we see throughout the investment cycle. The key thing is that there is almost always a "hot" sector that is the current darling on Wall Street. That is what day traders depend on, not whether that sector is Internet stocks, biotech companies or cyclicals.

Here again, the outlook appears to be conducive to a wave of growth ahead, as electronic network technology makes it possible to provide low-cost, real-time access to more and more financial markets and bring all world markets closer and closer together. Day traders, in the near future, are likely to have access to a world of investment choices.

All products are going to become electronically connected and traded in the future. The trend is clear. We see initiatives and pilot projects involving everything from bonds to commodities like grains and futures, and to foreign stocks. The key development for day traders and individuals will be which of those systems are truly designed to provide open access and a level playing field. Fair access to information is the key; knowing who the buyers and sellers are. It's not just ease of execution electronically; it's going to be access to the knowledge and information of who's buying and selling.

At Tradescape.com we're participating in one project that may show just how close we are to being able to give individuals access to the global world financial market that is open somewhere 24 hours a day.

The NASDAQ market and the Japanese company Softbank recently announced plans for a project to create a new Nasdaq style stock market. With the first phase starting as soon as next year, Japanese investors will ultimately be able to trade U.S. stocks listed on NASDAQ and U.S. investors will be able to trade Japanese stocks, all at one forum, and all on the Internet. Softbank is an investor in Tradescape.com, and one of the reasons for this investment was Tradescape.com's experience developing technology for swiftly and automatically choosing the best route for executing orders. Creating these networks of virtual exchanges begins the process of creating a true 24-hour, global, financial network able to efficiently match buyers and sellers.

While the growth and integration of financial markets will provide new opportunities for day trading, the opportunities are likely to expand even further as day traders borrow investment techniques from other disciplines and adapt them for day trading. We have seen some limited examples of progressive day traders adopting investment styles long used by hedge funds, for example. These include market neutral strategies where long and short positions are combined to take away the risk from an overall market jolt that could come in response to some economic news or event. That allows the investor to focus on trades designed to isolate and capture the discrepancy in performance that ought to appear between a stronger stock and a weaker stock. We have seen some limited examples of day traders using automated execution systems so that when they see certain types of opportunities, they can enter 10 orders or 50 orders designed to exploit that opportunity, instead of just having time to execute one or two. With more powerful technology, constructing these kind of individual program trading strategies should be amplified and become more prevalent.

We also expect to see increased opportunities to use technology for simulation, testing and research. There will be opportunities to try out multiple strategies in a virtual market lab, or test the impact of alternative strategic enhancements to a technique.

In conclusion, nimble traders have always exhibited an ability to tweak and adjust their strategies to the market. It is the nature of markets that one indicator might be almost unfailingly accurate in signaling direction for a few months, then suddenly be ignored by the market. A particular stock may be the bellwether in the spring, and ignored as a disappointing laggard by year end. The market's tenor can be bullish and shrug off countless pieces of bad news, then turn bearish and refuse to rally despite a string of positive reports. Trading patterns shift and change for various stocks and favorite investment themes

The need to learn these patterns and stay in tune with them is the reason that successful day trading can be an all-consuming passion. The successful players approach trading as a serious, full-time profession. Successful trading requires this approach. This is not something that a person is likely to take up as a hobby, something to spend two or three hours a week on as entertainment.

So, how can I answer the most important question that someone reading this book may have: How can a person know if they would be a successful day trader, able to take advantage of all the growing opportunities the field possesses?

Right now, the main body of successful traders I have met are people in their early to mid-20s. It is too early in the development of this business to say whether there are characteristics about the intensity and focus required that make trading primarily a young person's occupation. Wall Street's own trading floors have historically operated that way. Perhaps successful day traders will build up capital in their 20s that allows them to pursue other dreams, such as starting their own businesses as I did, which will take them through their 30s and beyond.

Another possibility is that this is simply a reflection of how a new business starts to grow, first becoming popular with a group of prime customers before becoming more established and with a much more diverse base of participants. New and unfamiliar technologies are most easily embraced by the young, who haven't spent a career learning other methods and approaches. Clearly there is a relation between the intensity of trading on screen and video game culture. The Nintendo generation is growing up and doesn't have to put away it's toys.

But as we have seen, with the PC and many other technology products, what begins as the province of a select few enthusiasts can grow and expand to become a widely adopted norm.

When we look at the early successful traders, who share a lot of outward similarities because they are from the same generation, it is tempting to think we can identify a series of traits that contribute to a trader's success. Wouldn't it be great to know in advance if you were going to succeed, or at least had the odds on your side?

Well, do you want to hear the good news or the bad news? Let's start with the bad news. The bad news is that there doesn't seem to be any way to predict in advance who will succeed at trading. Successful traders seem to share a passion, a hunger, an aggressiveness and a number of other traits that we see time and time again. They feel that way about trading. They may or may not feel that way about anything else. I've seen people who seem to fit the exact prototype, but when they start trying to trade, their style and approach changes completely. I've seen people who don't outwardly exhibit any of the personality traits I associate with a top trader, until the first time that they sit down at a terminal to invest.

That's the bad news. It is also the good news. Anyone can be a great trader. Anyone could be able to move into this and make a successful career for himself or herself.

This brings us back to something I said earlier about trading requiring full-time dedication, like any profession. There is an exception that we have seen in a few cases. There are people who have learned and mastered trading and who are able to continue doing it during short periods each day, or a few weeks out of the year when they take a break from other careers.

With trading, people like this don't have to make trade-offs. If there is a career or avocation that is their first love, they can pursue it, while still using trading to augment their opportunities. Or they can trade while they take time off from their other pursuits—a trading vacation. With wireless network technology advancing rapidly, a combination of the beach, trading, and tropical island nights may be a life some traders will be able to fashion for themselves in the very near future.

ELECTRONIC TRADING TERMS

Bid Price a market maker or investor who subscribes to an ECN is willing to pay for a NASDAQ stock.

Bounce A redirection in the market that occurs when there is a serious down movement followed by a serious upswing.

Covering the position Closing a position by buying back the stock that a trader sold short.

ECN (Electronic Communication Network) Investors presented on bid and offer of stock that purchase and sell the stocks in which they are trading. ECNs sometimes represent market makers, but they are not subjected to SOES. They only accept Preference orders.

Flat Net value equals zero. This is used to refer to profits and positions currently held.

High Bid   When a MM or ECN wants to pay higher for a stock than anyone else and increases the current bid price. The high bid is the act of increasing the bid price.

Hit the Bids   Term used when a trader wants to sell a stock on the bid.

Inside Market   The current price range of a stock. It is shown as the current bid by the current offer.

Low Offer   When a MM or ECN wants to sell a stock lower than anyone else and lowers the current offer price. The low offer is the act of decreasing the offer price.

Market Maker (MM)   NASD member firm that is present on the bid and offer of stocks. They make the market by quoting a bid and offer and the honor that quote. They are subject to SOES and Preference orders. Most are large institutional brokerages.

Offer   Price a market maker or investor who subscribes to an ECN is willing to sell a NASDAQ stock.

Overlying Offer   List of MMs and ECNs that are offering to sell the stock, but are not on the current offer.

Preference Order   Order to buy or sell that is only entered to and seen by a specific MM or ECN and is not open for anyone else to see or to execute.

Resistance Level   A level where a stock tends to receive resistance (mainly while it is going up). Once it reaches the level, the stock tends to stop going up and be resisted at that level of offers.

SOES   (Small Order Execution System) Trading system that allows investors to purchase and sell stocks immediately after they enter an order. The number one benefit is immediate executions.

SOES'ed Out   term for entering a SOES order and not receiving a print (execution).

Spread   The difference in price between the offer and bid of a stock. (Offer-Bid=Spread)

Support Level   A level where a stock tends to receive support (mainly while it is going down). Once it reaches the level, the stock tends to stop going down and be supported at that level of bids.

Swing   A sudden and dramatic redirection of the market.

Take the Offers   Term used when a trader wants to buy a stock on the offer.

Underlying Bid   List of MMs and ECNs that are willing to buy the stock but are not on the current bid.

INDEX

ABOUT THE AUTHORS

Jonathan R. Aspatore
Jonathan R. Aspatore is the founder of EPS Business Partners (www.epsbp.com), the parent company of ebrandedbooks.com, which provides entrepreneurial solutions to companies world-wide. He has written numerous books on entrepreneurial thinking and new business development in addition to being a monthly columnist for numerous web sites and publications. Jonathan began his career with Morgan Stanley in New York after studying entrepreneurial management in the Wharton School of Business. After working as an Investment Banker in the technology sector and in the Derivatives Product Group at Morgan Stanley, he went on to start EPS Business Partners in 1997. For any comments or questions, please contact him at aspatore@epsbp.com.

L. Adrienne Wichard
Adrienne Wichard is an editor and writer at Foofoo.com, a recently launched online magazine. She graduated from the University of Virginia with a degree in English language and literature.

Alicia Abell
Alicia Abell is an associate editor and writer at Washingtonian magazine. She graduated from Dartmouth College with a degree in English literature.